BE QUOTED

Be Quoted

From A to Z with Warren W. Wiersbe

EDITED BY JAMES R. ADAIR

Baker Books

A Division of Baker Book House Co
Grand Rapids, Michigan 49516

Published by Baker Books
a division of Baker Book House Company
P.O. Box 6287, Grand Rapids, MI 49516-6287

Printed in the United States of America

Library of Congress Cataloging-in-Publication Data

Wiersbe, Warren W.
    Be quoted : from A to Z with Warren W. Wiersbe / edited by James R. Adair.
        p.   cm.
    Includes index.
    ISBN 0-8010-1191-4 (hardcover)
    1. Wiersbe, Warren W.—Quotations. 2. Christian life—Quotations, maxims, etc. 3. Theology, Doctrinal—Quotations, maxims, etc. I. Adair, James R., 1923– II. Title.

BR1725.W449 A25 2000
230'.61—dc21   00-023103

For information about academic books, resources for Christian leaders, and all new releases available from Baker Book House, visit our web site:
                http://www.bakerbooks.com

CONTENTS

7

PREFACE

Welcome to a treasure chest of golden nuggets from the writings of my longtime friend, Warren Wiersbe. This is the third book I have produced related to his writings. The others are *A Time to Be Renewed* and *Through the Year with Warren W. Wiersbe.* I am honored to have been asked to compile this book of selected quotations from most of his books.

Warren and I began working together about 1970, soon after I got the assignment to start the Victor Books Division of Scripture Press Publications, then in Wheaton, Illinois, now merged with Cook Communications Ministries, Colorado Springs. He had written a study paperback on 1 John at the suggestion of Henry Jacobsen, editor of adult curriculum for Vacation Bible School use. It was published as one of Victor's first books. Warren's working title was *On Being a Real Christian,* but, as I recall, a liberal preacher already had a book with that title, or something similar, and the title was changed to *Be Real.*

Anxious to keep Warren writing for Victor, I encouraged him to write another study book for our planned Sunday school elective series, which helped in a big way to launch Victor Books. He obliged by writing a delightful study on Philippians. We decided to go with a "Be" title again, and thus his second book became *Be Joyful.* Happily, he is still writing "Be" books, until today the "Be" series covers all of the New Testament, plus many of the Old Testament, forty-two to date. Their total print is more than five million, including many foreign translations.

I personally had some qualms about the title of this book, fearing it might be mistaken for part of the Victor series. But, obviously, it isn't a study book per se. It's one of a kind. It's, as mentioned, a collection of gems from not only his many "Be" books but from almost all of his other books. Here is what I consider the cream of his writings, as quotations go, from A to Z!

I used to hear that many preachers across the land used Warren Wiersbe writings as the basis for sermons. And I'm sure that many still do. How extensive that was and is, nobody knows; but Warren has always considered it a compliment.

Now preachers and others will, we believe, find this book useful for selecting quotations to buttress points in messages. Other readers will, we believe, find this book stimulating. Many will find it helpful in devotional times. Each nugget will give you food for thought, something to chew on.

Lest you think I personally read all of Warren's books to select quotations, I didn't. I scanned many of his books; passages jumped out at me—many more, actually, than could be contained in this 208-page book. I also got expert help—from Dr. Erwin Rudolph, retired professor of English Literature, Wheaton College, and Vic Pearson, an environmental consultant with Fermilab, Aurora, Illinois, who was in seminary with Warren Wiersbe way back in the early '50s. Both men examined numerous books and marked pages for possible use. A big thanks to both of my good friends! Both reported they were greatly blessed in reading the assigned books.

You, too, I predict, will be blessed as you carefully read this book.

James R. Adair

Key to Sources

A Be Amazed (Minor Prophets)
B Be Available (Judges)
C Be Comforted (Isaiah)
D Be Committed (Ruth and Esther)
E Be Concerned (Minor Prophets)
F Be Decisive (Jeremiah)
G Be Determined (Nehemiah)
H Be God's Guest
I Be Heroic (Minor Prophets)
J Be Holy (Leviticus)
K Being a Child of God
L Be Obedient (Abraham)
M Be Patient (Job)
N Be Satisfied (Ecclesiastes)
O Be Skillful (Proverbs)
P Be Strong (Joshua)
Q Be What You Are
R Comforting the Bereaved
S When Life Falls Apart
T Enjoy Your Freedom
U Five Secrets of Living
V From Worry to Worship
W God Isn't in a Hurry
X Be Mature (James)
Y His Name Is Wonderful
Z In Praise of Plodders!
AA Jesus and Your Sorrows
BB Jesus' Seven Last Words
CC Key Words of the Christian Life
DD Live Like a King
EE Lonely People
FF Meet Your Conscience
GG Meet Yourself in the Psalms
HH On Being a Servant of God

II Prayer: Basic Training
JJ Prayer, Praise, and Promises (Psalms)
KK Preaching and Teaching with Imagination
LL Put Your Life Together
MM Run with the Winners
NN Scriptures That Sing
OO Something Happens When Churches Pray
PP So That's What a Christian Is!
QQ Ten Power Principles for Christian Service
RR The Bible Exposition Commentary, Vol. 1
SS The Bible Exposition Commentary, Vol. 2
TT The Bumps Are What You Climb On
UU The Cross of Jesus
VV The Elements of Preaching
WW The Integrity Crisis
XX The Intercessory Prayer of Jesus
YY The Most Expensive Thing in the World
ZZ The Names of Jesus
AAA The Strategy of Satan
BBB Be Rich
CCC Thoughts for Men on the Move
DDD What Shall We Name the Baby?
EEE Windows on the Parables
FFF With the Word
GGG What to Wear to the War

Abide/Abiding

What does it mean to "abide"? It means to keep in fellowship with Christ so that His life can work in and through us to produce fruit. This certainly involves the Word of God and the confession of sin so that nothing hinders our communion with Him (John 15:3). It also involves obeying Him because we love Him (John 15:9–10).

How can we tell when we are "abiding in Christ"? Is there a special feeling? No, but there are special evidences that appear and they are unmistakably clear. For one thing, when you are abiding in Christ, you produce fruit (John 15:2). Also, you experience the Father's "pruning" so that you will bear more fruit (John 15:2). The believer who is abiding in Christ has his prayers answered (John 15:7) and experiences a deepening love for Christ and for other believers (John 15:9, 12–13). He also experiences joy (John 15:11).

This abiding relationship is natural to the branch and the vine, but it must be cultivated in the Christian life. It is not automatic. Abiding in Christ demands worship, meditation on God's Word, prayer, sacrifice, and service—but what a joyful experience it is!

RR–355

The more we abide in Christ, the more fruit we bear; and the more fruit we bear, the more the Father has to prune us so that the quality keeps up with the quantity. Left to itself, the branch might produce many clusters, but they will be inferior in quality. God is glorified by a bigger crop that is also a *better* crop.

RR–356

"Whosoever abides in Him does not sin" (1 John 3:6 NKJV). "Abide" is one of John's favorite words. To *abide* in Christ means to be in fellowship with Him, to allow nothing to come between ourselves and Christ. *Sonship* (being born of God) brings about our *union* with Christ; but *fellowship* makes possible our *communion* with Christ that keeps us from deliberately disobeying His Word.

A person who deliberately and habitually sins is proving that he does not know Christ and therefore cannot be abiding in Him.

SS–505

Have you ever wondered why some believers seem to "sail through life" in constant sunshine, while others experience suffering and loss? To be sure, God has different plans for each of His children; but this much is true: *believers who abide in Christ can expect to suffer.* The Father's knife is ready to cut away anything in their lives that is keeping them from bearing more fruit for His glory. The Father may *hurt* you, but He will never *harm* you. His pruning is for your good and His glory, and that is all that really counts.

U–39

Prayer is also a part of abiding. "If you abide in Me, and My words abide in you, ask whatever you wish, and it shall be done for you" (John 15:7 NASB). The better we know the Word of God, the better we can pray; for the Word of God reveals the will of God. "And this is the confidence which we have before Him, that, if we ask anything according to His will, He hears us" (1 John 5:14 NASB). Of course, prayer is much more

than asking. It also involves giving thanks, expressing love and worship, and also confessing sin.

U–32

Adoption

The Holy Spirit is also "the Spirit of adoption" (Rom. 8:14–17 NASB). The word *adoption* in the New Testament means "being placed as an adult son." We come into God's family by birth. But the instant we are born into the family, God adopts us and gives us the position of an adult son. A baby cannot walk, speak, make decisions, or draw on the family wealth. But the believer can do all of these the instant he is born again.

RR–540

Advocate

Christ also ministers as our Advocate (1 John 2:1). As our High Priest, Jesus gives us grace to keep us from sinning. As our Advocate, He restores us when we confess our sins. His ministry in heaven makes possible our ministry of witness on earth, through the power of the Spirit.

RR–365

Alcohol

Most of the advertisements that promote the sale of alcoholic bev-

14

erages depict fashionable people in gracious settings, giving the subtle impression that "social drinking" and success are synonymous. But pastors, social workers, physicians, and dedicated members of Alcoholics Anonymous would paint a different picture. They've seen firsthand the wrecked marriages, ruined bodies and minds, abused families, and shattered careers that often accompany what people call "social drinking."

Longtime baseball coach and manager Connie Mack said that alcohol had no more place in the human body than sand had in the gas tank of an automobile. Alcohol is a narcotic, not a food; it destroys, not nourishes. The Bible warns against drunkenness (Prov. 20:1; 21:17; 23:20–21, 29–35; Isa. 5:11; Luke 21:34; Rom. 13:13–14; 1 Cor. 5:11; Eph. 5:18; 1 Peter 4:3–5); and even the *Koran* says, "There is a devil in every berry of the grape."

The best way to avoid drunkenness is not to drink at all. A Japanese proverb warns, "First the man takes a drink, then the drink takes a drink, and then the drink takes the man." And King Lemuel's mother taught him, "It is not for kings, O Lemuel, it is not for kings to drink wine; nor for princes strong drink" (Prov. 31:4).

D–77

Altar

We may set aside places in our church buildings and call them altars; but they are really not altars in the biblical sense. Why? Because Christ's sacrifice has already been made, once and for all; and the gifts that we bring to God are acceptable, not because of any earthly altar, but because of a heavenly altar, Jesus Christ.

SS–329

Anger

Unrighteous anger feeds the ego and produces the poison of selfishness in the heart.

A–92

I have read that one out of every thirty-five deaths in Chicago is a murder, and that most of these murders are "crimes of passion" caused by anger among friends or relatives. Jesus did not say that anger leads to murder; He said that anger *is* murder.

There is a holy anger against sin (Eph. 4:26), but Jesus talked about an unholy anger against people. The word He used in Matthew 5:22 means "a settled anger, malice that is nursed inwardly." Jesus described a sinful experience that involved several stages. First there was *causeless anger.* This anger then exploded

15

into *words:* "Raca—empty-headed person!" These words added fuel to the fire so that the person said, "You fool—rebel!"

Anger is such a foolish thing. It makes us destroyers instead of builders. It robs us of freedom and makes us prisoners. To hate someone is to commit murder in our hearts (1 John 3:15).

SS–24

Many church fights are the result of short tempers and hasty words. There is a godly anger against sin (Eph. 4:26); and if we love the Lord, we must hate sin (Ps. 97:10). But man's anger does not produce God's righteousness (James 1:20). In fact, anger is just the opposite of the patience God wants to produce in our lives as we mature in Christ (James 1:3–4).

SS–347

Antinomianism (or Legalism)

In our desire to escape "legalism," I fear we have embraced a subtle form of antinomianism (the idea that salvation by grace negates our obligation to moral law), with results that would have driven our fathers to their knees in prayer: treating the marriage covenant lightly, adopting the lifestyle of "the rich and famous," using the world's approach in mer-

chandising the gospel, ignoring the Lord's Day, refusing to enforce standards, and even watering down our preaching so people won't be offended.

WW–61

But this blood-bought freedom doesn't give Christians the right to reject the law of God and deliberately disobey it. The word for this is *antinomianism*—"against the law." Legalism is bad enough, but antinomianism is worse, for it turns liberty into license and makes God's law our enemy instead of our servant.

K–158

Appreciation

Appreciation is great medicine for the soul.

SS–105

Armor of God

We are never out of reach of Satan's devices, so we must never be without the whole armor of God.

SS–59

Since we are fighting against enemies in the spirit world, we need special equipment both for offense and defense. God has provided the "whole armor" for us (see Eph. 6:13–17), and we dare not

16

omit any part. Satan looks for that unguarded area where he can get a beachhead (Eph. 4:27). Paul commanded his readers to put on the armor, take the weapons, and withstand Satan, all of which we do by faith. Knowing that Christ has already conquered Satan, and that the spiritual armor and weapons are available, by faith we accept what God gives us and go out to meet the foe. The day is evil, and the enemy is evil, but "if God be for us, who can be against us?" (Rom. 8:31).

SS–58

Arrogant/Arrogance

How does an arrogant attitude affect a believer's relationship with God? It is as though he trods Jesus Christ underfoot, cheapens the precious blood that saved him ("an unholy thing" [Heb. 10:29] = "a common thing"), and insults the Holy Spirit. This is just the opposite of the exhortation given in Hebrews 10:19–25! Instead of having a bold profession of faith, hope, and love, a backslidden believer so lives that his actions and attitudes bring disgrace to the name of Christ and the church.

What can this kind of a Christian expect from God? He can expect severe discipline. (Chastening is the theme of Heb. 12.)

SS–316

Ascension

The church's authority, the church's ministry and the church's energy are all based on the ascension of Jesus Christ. This brings us to Acts 1 where we find the local church meeting together in prayer. "These all continued with one accord in prayer and supplication" (v. 14). The church's activity is based on the ascension of our Lord Jesus Christ. He went back to heaven. He promised to send the Holy Spirit. What is the link between heaven and earth? Prayer. When a Christian prays, he is claiming His authority. When a Christian prays, he is sharing in His ministry. When a Christian prays, he is receiving divine energy.

OO–14

The church's authority comes from the ascended Christ. The church's ministry comes from the ascended Christ. The church's energy comes from the ascended Christ. Therefore, the church's activity ought to be praying to the ascended Christ, worshiping Him, asking Him to release His power in us so that by His authority we might be involved in His ministry.

OO–15

Assurance

What is the good news to sinners today? It is the assurance that Jesus Christ has fully met the demands of God's law. He has paid for your sins on the cross, and offers to you the spiritual riches that only He can give.

Y–102

Our confidence that we are God's children comes from the witness of the Word of God before us and the witness of the Spirit of God within us (1 John 5:9–13). However, the assurance of salvation isn't based only on what we know from the Bible or how we feel in our hearts. It's also based on how we live; for if there hasn't been a change in our behavior, then it's doubtful that we've truly been born again (2 Cor. 5:21; James 2:14–26).

P–39

Astrology

As for astrology and the influence of heavenly bodies, Paul denounced this with vigor. On the cross, Jesus won a complete victory over all satanic powers (Col. 2:15). Christians do not need to turn to the rudiments of the world (Col. 2:8, 20). This word translated *rudiments* means "elemental beings" or "elementary principles." In this case, it refers to the beings that (according to the gnostics) controlled the heavenly bodies that in turn controlled events on earth. Believers who consult horoscopes substitute superstition for revelation and deny the person and work of Christ.

SS–103

Attitude

If your life is falling apart, it is likely that you are part of the problem. We have seen that unbelief, rebellion, and bitterness only lead to emptiness. You can continue to tear things apart by your bad attitude, or you can change your life for the better by submitting to God and allowing Him to work.

LL–46

Outlook determines outcome, and attitude determines action.

X–22

David discovered that what was important was not the *circumstances around him but the attitude within him.*

JJ–day 3

Authority

When Jesus sent His disciples out to minister, He first gave them the authority they needed to do the job; and He promised to meet their

18

every need (Matt. 10:1–15). As we go forth to serve the Lord, we have behind us all authority in heaven and on earth (28:18); so we don't have to be afraid. The important thing is that we go where He sends us and that we do the work He has called us to do.

G–29

B

Babies

Babies are fragile, but God uses the weak things of the world to confound the mighty (1 Cor. 1:26–28). Babies must have time to grow up, but God is patient and is never late in accomplishing His will. Each baby God sends is a gift from God, a new beginning, and carries with it tremendous potential. What a tragedy that we live in a society that sees the unborn baby as a menace instead of a miracle, an intruder instead of an inheritance.

B–107

Backsliding

God offers to heal, not just the symptoms of backsliding, but the backsliding itself. The false prophets dealt only with symptoms and announced a false peace that gave the people a false confidence (Jer. 6:14; 7:8; 8:11). But a true physician of souls will tell the truth and seek to lead sinners to genuine spiritual healing that comes from honest confession and repentance.

This reminds me of a story I've often used in sermons. A certain church member was in the habit of closing his public prayers with "And, Lord, take the cobwebs out of my heart!" One of the other members became weary of this litany, so one evening, after hearing it again, he stood and prayed, "And, Lord, while You're at it . . . kill the spider!" Jeremiah was out to "kill the spider" and cure the patient.

F–31

Balance

Our Christian lives desperately need *balance*. Certainly we get to know God better as we pray in our private rooms and as we meditate on His Word. But we also get to know Him as we walk in our daily lives and work to win others and help His people.

SS–112

Baptism

When you trusted Jesus Christ as your Savior, the Holy Spirit of God baptized you into the Body of Christ. This baptism did not occur after conversion but was simultaneous with conversion (1 Cor. 12:13). Every believer has the gift of the Holy Spirit, and every believer has been identified with Jesus Christ in His death, burial, resurrection, and ascension. This is the beautiful truth of Romans 6. This is why Paul said, "What shall we say then? Shall we continue in sin, that grace may abound? God forbid" (vv. 1–2). After all we have experienced in Jesus Christ, how can we continue in sin?

T–44

The Corinthians made too much of baptism. "I was baptized by Apollos!" one would boast, while another would say, "Oh, but I was baptized by Paul!"

It is wrong to identify any man's name with your baptism other than the name of Jesus Christ. To do so is to create division. I have read accounts about people who had to be baptized by a certain preacher, using special water (usually from the Jordan River), on a special day, as though these are the matters that are important! Instead of honoring the Lord Jesus Christ and promoting the unity of the church, these people exalt men and create disunity.

RR–570

Baptism by immersion (which is the illustration Paul uses in Rom. 6) pictures the believer's identification with Christ in His death, burial, and resurrection. It is an outward symbol of an inward experience. Paul is not saying that their immersion in water put them "into Jesus Christ," for that was accomplished by the Spirit when they believed. Their immersion was a picture of what the Spirit did: the Holy Spirit identified them with Christ in His death, burial, and resurrection.

RR–531

Battle, Battles

The battles we fight are not with flesh and blood on earth, but with satanic powers "in the heavenly realms" (Eph. 6:12 NIV).

SS–10

The first step toward winning the battle and claiming our inheritance is to let God encourage us

and then for us to encourage others. A discouraged army is never
victorious.

"See, the Lord your God has
given you the land. Go up and take
possession of it as the Lord, the
God of your fathers, told you. Do
not be afraid; do not be discouraged" (Deut. 1:21 NIV).

Be strong! The battle is the
Lord's!

P-33

It is important to note that,
when Jesus took upon Him a
human body, He *permanently* became a part of the battle on earth.
And since His children are united
to Him through the Spirit, He is
able to empower them in their battle against Satan.

EEE-102

Beauty

Ephesus was a wealthy com-
mercial city, and some women
there competed against each other
for attention and popularity. In that
day expensive hairdos arrayed with
costly jewelry were an accepted
way to get to the top socially. Paul
admonished the Christian women
to major on the "inner person," the
true beauty that only Christ can
give. He did not forbid the use of
nice clothing or ornaments. He
urged balance and propriety, with
the emphasis on modesty and holy
character.

"It's getting harder and harder for
a Christian woman to find the right
kind of clothes!" a church member
complained to me one summer. "I
refuse to wear the kind of swimsuits
they're selling! I simply won't go
swimming. Whatever happened to
old-fashioned modesty?"

Paul did not suggest that good
works are a substitute for clothing!
Rather, he was contrasting the
"cheapness" of expensive clothes
and jewelry with the true values of
godly character and Christian service. "Godliness" is another key word
in Paul's pastoral letters (1 Tim. 2:2,
10; 3:16; 4:7–8; 6:3, 5–6, 11; 2 Tim.
3:5; Titus 1:1). Glamor can be par-
tially applied on the outside, but
godliness must come from within.

XX-00

Belief

What we believe determines how
we behave, and both determine
what we become. If we believe the
truth, the truth will sanctify us (see
John 17:17) and set us free (see John
8:31–32). If we believe lies, we will
gradually *become a lie* as we lose our
integrity and begin to practice
duplicity. It's a fundamental principle that we will become like the god
we worship.

WW-60

"Betweener"

I once heard a preacher say, "Most Christians are 'betweeners.'"

"What do you mean by that?" I asked.

"They are between Egypt and Canaan—out of the place of danger, but not yet into the place of rest and rich inheritance," he replied. "They are between Good Friday and Easter Sunday—saved by the blood but not yet enjoying newness of resurrection life."

Are *you* a "betweener"?

SS–295

Bible

Blessed is the Bible student who comes to God's Word with an open mind, a loving heart, a submissive will, *and a sensitive imagination.*

KK–29

God gives us a compass and a Book of promises and principles—the Bible—and lets us make our decisions day by day as we sense the leading of His Spirit. *This is how we grow.*

Y–27–28

A father took his son to a large city museum, thinking that the visit would entertain the boy. But for two hours the lad did nothing but sigh and complain. Finally in desperation he said to his father, "Dad, let's go someplace where *things are real!"*

Some people feel that way when they read the Bible. They think they are in a religious museum, looking at ancient artifacts that have no meaning for life in today's scientific world. *But they are wrong.* No book published has more meaning for our lives, and more relevance to our problems, than the Bible. No wonder William Lyon Phelps, for years called "Yale's most inspiring professor," said: "I believe a knowledge of the Bible without a college course is more valuable than a college course without a Bible."

SS–156

I have noticed that some church officers know their church constitutions better than they know the Word of God. While it is good to have bylaws and regulations that help maintain order, it is important to manage the affairs of a church on the basis of the Word of God. The Scriptures were the "constitution" of the early church! A deacon who does not know the Bible is an obstacle to progress in a local assembly.

SS–220

We are not saved by believing the Bible (see John 5:39), but by trusting the Christ who is revealed in the Bible. Satan knows the Bible but he is not saved. Timothy was raised on the Holy Scriptures in a godly home. Yet it was not until Paul led him to Christ that he was saved.

What is the relationship of the Bible to salvation? To begin with, the Bible reveals our need for salvation. It is a mirror that shows us how filthy we are in God's sight. The Bible explains that every lost sinner is condemned *now* (John 3:18–21) and needs a Saviour *now*. It also makes it clear that a lost sinner cannot save himself.

But the Bible also reveals God's wonderful plan of salvation: Christ died for our sins! If we trust Him, He will save us (John 3:16–18). The Bible also helps give us the assurance of our salvation (see 1 John 5:9–13). Then the Bible becomes our spiritual food to nourish us that we might grow in grace and serve Christ. It is our sword for fighting Satan and overcoming temptation.

SS–252

The purpose of Bible study is *not* just to understand doctrines or to be able to defend the faith, as important as these things are. The ultimate purpose is the equipping of the believers who read it. It is the Word of God that equips God's people to do the work of God.

SS–253

Bible Study

Unfortunately, what some people call "Bible study" is too often just a group of unprepared people exchanging their ignorance.

RR–218

Bitterness

Bitterness refers to a settled hostility that poisons the whole inner man.

SS–42

Bitterness and anger, usually over trivial things, make havoc of homes, churches, and friendships.

SS–43

Blasphemy

But what is this terrible "sin against the Holy Spirit" called blasphemy? Can it be committed today, and, if so, how? Our Lord said that God will forgive evil words spoken against the Son, but not against the Spirit. Does this mean that the Holy Spirit is more important than Jesus Christ, God's Son? Surely not. We often hear the name of God or Jesus Christ used in blasphemy, but rarely if ever the name of the Holy Spirit. How can God forgive words spoken against His Son, and yet not forgive words spoken against the Spirit?

It appears that this situation existed *only while Christ was ministering on earth*. Jesus did not appear to be different from any other Jewish man (Isa. 53:2). To speak against Christ could be forgiven *while He was on earth*. But when the Spirit of God came at Pentecost as proof that Jesus was the Christ, and was alive, to reject the witness of the Spirit was final. The only consequence would be judgment.

When the leaders rejected John the Baptist, they were rejecting *the Father* who sent him. When they rejected Jesus, they were rejecting *the Son*. But when they rejected the ministry of the Apostles, they rejected *the Holy Spirit*—and that is the end. There is no more witness. Such rejection cannot be forgiven.

RR–43

Bless, Blessing

God doesn't franchise His blessings the way companies franchise their products to local dealers. You can't go to Bethel and Gilgal (see Amos 4:4) or to Beersheba and go home with a blessing in your baggage. Unless we personally meet the Lord, deal with our inner spiritual life, and seek His face, our hearts will never be transformed.

E–47

We can avoid a great many heartaches in this life by isolating ourselves from the rest of the world. If we refuse to talk to others, to become involved in Sunday school or church, to visit the sick and the grieving, to read or watch the news to see what is happening in the world, or to listen to the announcements in church to find out who may be hurting, we can escape a great deal of suffering. But by ignoring the cares of others, we will also miss many blessings and will rob ourselves of the privilege of being a blessing.

NN–29

I have felt for a long time that one of the particular temptations of the maturing Christian is the danger of getting accustomed to his blessings. Like the world traveler who has been everywhere and seen everything, the maturing Christian is in danger of taking his blessings for granted and getting so accustomed to them that they fail to excite him as they once did.

The best cure for the sin of getting accustomed to our blessings is this: Constantly give thanks to God for all He gives and all He does. A thankful heart, lost in the wonder of God's grace and goodness, will never take God's blessings for

25

granted. Just as a little child is constantly filled with wonder at what life brings him, so the maturing believer must marvel at God's gifts and God's provisions.

W–77, 79

God desires to bless us, but we must meet His conditions for receiving blessings. By staying separate from the world and keeping saturated in the Word, we may expect God's blessings. Resolve to meditate on the Word of God and obey it. He will make you a blessing to others.

JJ–2

God does not need our blessing, but we need to bless God! We should bless Him for what He is, the living God who meets us in grace and cares for our every need, spiritual and material. As we bless the Lord from submissive and grateful hearts, we grow spiritually; and as we grow, we discover more of His blessings—and we praise Him more! Worship and praise are the thermometer of the spiritual life. If our hearts are cold and complaining, we will be silent, like the dead; but if our hearts are warm and appreciative, we will praise and bless God wherever we are.

GG–31

Blind

No one is so blind as he who will not see, the one who thinks he has "all truth" and there is nothing more for him to learn (John 9:28, 34).

RR–327

Blood

We need no proof that the blood of Jesus Christ is far superior to that of animal sacrifices. How can the blood of *animals* ever solve the problem of *humans'* sins? Jesus Christ became a Man that He might be able to die for people's sins. His death was voluntary; it is doubtful that any Old Testament sacrifice volunteered for the job! An animal's blood was carried by the high priest into the holy of holies, but Jesus Christ presented *Himself* in the presence of God as the final and complete sacrifice for sins. Of course, the animal sacrifices were repeated, while Jesus Christ offered Himself but once. Finally, no animal sacrifices ever purchased "eternal redemption." Their blood could only "cover" sin until the time when Christ's blood would take away sin (John 1:29). We have "eternal redemption." It is not conditioned on our merit or good works; it is secured once and for all by the finished work of Jesus Christ.

SS–310

Through Jesus Christ, we who are sinners can enter into the holy of holies in the heavenly sanctuary (Heb. 10:19–22). Physically, of course, we are on earth; but spiritually, we are communing with God in the heavenly holy of holies. In order for God to receive us into this heavenly fellowship, the blood of Jesus Christ *had to be applied.* We enter into God's presence "by the blood of Jesus" (Heb. 10:19).

The Old Covenant was established by blood, and so was the New Covenant. But the New Covenant was established on the basis of a better sacrifice, applied in a better place! The patterns (types) were purified by the blood of animals, but the original sanctuary was purified by the blood of the Son of God. This was a far more costly sacrifice.

SS–311–12

Body

God wants you to give Him your body. That sounds very ordinary, but it's one of the most spiritual things you can do! If God is going to use you, He must have your body. When Jesus Christ came to earth to redeem us, He had to have a body. In order to get His message of salvation to a wicked world, Jesus Christ must have a Body—the church. God can use my fingers to write letters. He can use my feet to make visits in homes. He can use my lips to speak the message of truth. That's why you should take good care of your body—it's the only tool you've got. A person would be a fool to pour sand into his gas tank, wouldn't he? He would wreck the car. Well, people do some foolish things with their bodies. God wants your body as a holy sacrifice, as a complete sacrifice to Him. Just as Jesus gave His body on the cross for you, God wants you to give your body on the altar for Him.

T–50

We as believer-priests have the wonderful privilege of caring for God's dwelling place. This begins with the care of our own bodies, which are the temple of God. A Christian should no more defile his body than a Jew would defile the temple or the tabernacle. Caring for one's body is much more than showing good sense or even practicing good health. It is an act of worship and service to the Lord who lives within (Rom. 12:1–2).

PP–72

27

Books, Devotional

Finally, what about the use of devotional books? Having written several of them myself, I do feel they have an important ministry, but never as substitutes for your Bible. If I use a devotional book, it's always after I've done my meditating and praying, not before. Use a devotional book that has some substance to it, one that helps you better understand God's Word for yourself. Reading a Bible verse, a story, and a poem, plus a "thought for the day," is like gulping down fast food and not taking time for a balanced meal. Eating fast food is better than starving; but if it takes away your appetite for satisfying meals that give you what you need, it's doing you more harm than good. You don't want to live on substitutes.

K–68

Brokenhearted

God can heal the brokenhearted—if all the pieces are given to Him.

R–27

Build, Builders

All of us are builders and we must be careful to build wisely. To "build on the rock" simply means to obey what God commands in His Word. To "build on the sand" means to give Christ lip service, but not obey His will. It may look as if we are building a strong house, but if it has no foundation, it cannot last.

RR–194

Anyone can go through life as a destroyer; God has called His people to be builders. What an example Nehemiah is to us! Trace his "so" statements and see how God used him: "So I prayed" (2:4); "So I came to Jerusalem" (v. 11); "So they strengthened their hands for this good work" (v. 18); "So built we the wall" (4:6); "So we labored in the work" (v. 21); "So the wall was finished" (6:15).

G–35

Busy

Our world is a busy world. We have little time to pause, contemplate, and wonder. Even vacationers pause only long enough to take photos or make videos that they can look at back home when they have more time. They don't have time to get close to people or God's creation, to stand and wonder at what He has made. Quick! Get a picture or two and buy some postcards. We have miles to cover before the day ends!

ZZ–21

28

You have probably noticed that God often speaks to His people and calls them while they are busy doing their daily tasks. Both Moses and David were caring for sheep, and Gideon was threshing wheat. Peter and his partners were mending nets when Jesus called them. It is difficult to steer a car when the engine is not running. When we get busy, God starts to direct us.

RR–171

C

Call

Moses said, "I am not" (Num. 11:14), but God's name is I AM. Whenever you say, "I am not," just remember God says, "I AM" (Exod. 3:14). God "is able to do exceedingly abundantly above all that we ask or think" (Eph. 3:20) because His calling is also His enabling. If God has called you, He will equip you. If God has called you, He will enlighten you. If God has called you, He will enable you. If God has called you, He will encourage you. He will see you through. Therefore, don't pray as Moses did, "Kill me. Take me away from my wretchedness" (see Num. 11:15). Instead, say, "Lord, You do the work, You get the glory. Give me what I need. Give me the divine enablement to glorify Your name," and God will see you through.

EE–47

If the Lord calls you, He will equip you for the task He wants you to fulfill. It has well been said "The will of God does not send you where the grace of God cannot keep you."

FFF–638

Cares

Christians do have cares and do experience suffering. It is an inescapable part of life. But we belong to a God who cares. He has promised to take care of us, and what He has promised He is able to do. We can cast our cares on Him, trusting Him to give us the courage, wisdom, grace, and strength to do what is required and to give us the faith to trust Him for the rest. Cast "all your care upon him; for he careth for you" (1 Peter 5:7).

NN–35

Not only do we have the Lord's promises, but His *providence* also proves that He cares. God is continually going before us and preparing the way. Nothing happens to the believer outside of the permissive, directive will of God. I'm encouraged to know that when I begin a new day, my Shepherd has already gone before me. One of the greatest assurances of God's providence is found in Romans 8:28: "And we know that all things work together for good to them that love God, to them who are the called according to his purpose."

NN–31

Change

When we are young, change is a treat; but as we grow older, change becomes a threat. But when Jesus Christ is in control of your life, you need never fear change or decay.

Y–63

Over the years I've seen churches and parachurch ministries flounder and almost destroy themselves in futile attempts to embalm the past and escape the future. Their theme song was, "As it was in the beginning, so shall it ever be, world without end." Often I've prayed with and for godly Christian leaders who were criticized, persecuted, and attacked simply because, like Joshua, they had a divine commission to lead a ministry into new fields of conquest; but the people would not follow. More than one pastor has been offered as a sacrificial lamb because he dared to suggest that the church make some changes.

P–22

It's unfortunate but true that sometimes the only way a ministry can move forward is by conducting a few funerals. A pastor friend of mine pleaded with his church board to build a new educational plant to house an exploding Sunday school. One of the longtime members of the board, a prominent businessman in the city, said to him, "You'll do this over my dead body!" *And they did!* A few days later, that officer had a heart attack and died; and the church moved ahead and built the much-needed educational plant.

P–30

Channels

We are not reservoirs, but channels of blessing, to share with others what God has graciously given to us.

RR–186

Character

Two indications of a person's character are what makes him laugh and what makes him weep.

SS–45

Character reveals itself in the hidden things of everyday life as well as the dramatic things of public ministry—things like telling the truth when a lie would help you escape trouble, taking the blame when somebody else deserves it, not cutting corners on a job that nobody will inspect, or making unnecessary sacrifices to help people who won't appreciate what you do anyway. Character means living your life before God, fearing only Him and seeking to please Him alone, no matter how you feel or what others may say or do.

QQ–21

Character is the raw material of life, out of which we either by diligence construct a temple or by negligence create a trash heap. Abraham Lincoln said that character was like a tree and reputation like a shadow of the tree. "The shadow is what we think of it," said Lincoln. "The tree is the real thing." Reputation is what people *think* we are; character is what God and the holy angels *know* we are. Evangelist D. L. Moody once said that character was "what a man is in the dark"; financial wizard J. P. Morgan called character the best collateral a person could give.

QQ–20

For the Christian, a healthy and holy character is formed by making Scripture a part of our inner being and obeying what it says. It comes from spending time faithfully in worship and prayer, gladly making sacrifices and willingly serving others. Character is strengthened when we suffer and depend on the grace of God to bring us through and glorify His name. It means saying with Job, "But he knows the way that I take; when he has tested me, I shall come forth as gold" (Job 23:10 NKJV). Character comes from discipline and devotion, from courage and commitment, from the myriad of things that Paul experienced and wrote about in 2 Corinthians 6:3–10 and 11:23–12:10.

QQ–21

God builds character in the disappointments of life and He also gives a witness. In the midst of his disappointments, Jeremiah bore witness to the Lord and gave His message to the people. . . . When you accept disappointments, trust God, and yield to Him, you leave something behind to help others in the battles of life.

TT–45

Life is built on character, and character is built on decisions. But decisions are based on values, *and values must be accepted by faith.* Moses made his life-changing decisions on the basis of values that other people thought were foolish (Heb. 11:24–29), but God honored his faith. The Christian enjoys all that God gives him (1 Tim. 6:17) because he lives "with eternity's values in view."

RR–193

Chastening

What does God do while a spiritual regression is going on? He keeps speaking to us, encouraging us to get back to the Word. If we fail to listen and obey, then He begins to chasten us. This chastening process is the theme of Hebrews 12, the climactic chapter in the epistle. "The Lord shall judge *His people*" (Heb. 10:30, italics mine). God does not allow His children to become "spoiled brats" by permitting them to willfully defy His Word. He always chastens in love.

SS–277

The fact that the Father chastens us is proof that we are maturing, and it is the means by which we can mature even more.

Chastening is the evidence of the Father's love. Satan wants us to believe that the difficulties of life are proof that God does *not* love us, but just the opposite is true. Sometimes God's chastening is seen in His *rebukes* from the Word or from circumstances. At other times He shows His love by *punishing* ("the Lord . . . scourgeth") us with some physical suffering. Whatever the experience, we can be sure that His chastening hand is controlled by His loving heart. The Father does not want us to be pampered babies; He wants us to become mature adult sons and daughters who can be trusted with the responsibilities of life.

SS–324

The important thing is how God's child responds to chastening. He can despise it or faint under it (Heb. 12:5), both of which are wrong. He should show reverence to the Father by submitting to His will (Heb. 12:9), using the experience to exercise himself spiritually (Heb. 12:11; 1 Tim. 4:7–8). Hebrews 12:12–13 sounds like a coach's orders to his team! Lift up your hands! Strengthen those knees (Isa. 35:3)! Get those lazy feet on the track (Prov. 4:26)! On your mark, get set, GO!

SS–325

It's a serious thing to enter into a covenant relationship with God, because He will always keep His Word, either to bless or to chasten. If we are the recipients of His love, then we can expect to be the recipients of His chastening if we disobey Him (Prov. 3:11–12). God is always faithful.

F–69

Children

Nowhere in the Bible is the training of children assigned to agencies outside the home, no matter how they might assist God.

SS–54

Home is the place where the children ought to learn about the Lord and the Christian life. It is time that Christian parents stop "passing the buck" to Sunday school teachers and Christian day-school teachers, and start nurturing their children.

SS–55

The child who does not learn to obey his parents is not likely to grow up obeying *any* authority. He will defy his teachers, the police, his employers, and anyone else who tries to exercise authority over him. The breakdown in authority in our society reflects the breakdown of authority in the home.

SS–143

Choices

You can make one of three choices when faced with a difficult situation because of your disobedience. You can blame God or someone else for your problems and try to cover up your sin; you can give up and return to your former, sinful life; or you can stand up, take responsibility for your actions, see God's forgiveness and trust in Him.

LL–29

Christian

A Christian is not somebody who tries to imitate Christ. A Christian is a person who is identified with Christ as a member of His body and the life of Christ flows in and through him. He has a living relationship with the glorified Son of God through the indwelling Spirit of God (1 Cor. 6:19–20; Gal. 2:20). This means he can have a life of spiritual vitality as he draws upon the strength of the Lord. The "Spirit of life in Christ Jesus" (Rom. 8:2) enables him to obey the will of God and produce fruit for His glory (Gal. 5:22–23).

PP–53

It was at Antioch that the name *Christian* was first applied to the disciples of Jesus Christ. The Latin suffix *ian* means "belonging to the party of." In derision, some of the pagan citizens of Antioch joined this Latin suffix to the Hebrew name "Christ" and came up with *Christian*. The name is found only three times in the entire New Testament: Acts 11:26; 26:28; 1 Peter 4:16.

Unfortunately, the word *Christian* has lost a great deal of significance over the centuries and no longer means "one who has turned from sin, trusted Jesus Christ, and received salvation by grace" (see Acts 11:21–23). Many people who have never been born again consider themselves "Christians" simply because they say they are not "pagans." After all, they may belong to a church, attend services somewhat regularly, and even occasionally give to the work of the church! But it takes more than that for a sinner to become a child of God. It takes repentance from sin and faith in Jesus Christ, who died for our sins on the cross and rose again to give us eternal life.

The believers in the early church *suffered* because they were Christians (1 Peter 4:16). Dr. David Otis Fuller has asked, "If you were arrested for being a Christian,

would there be enough evidence to convict you?" A good question! And the answer is a matter of life or death!

RR–450

Christian Life

The Christian life has two dimensions: faith toward God and love toward men, and you cannot separate the two.

SS–14

As God's chosen people, we're to live worthy of our calling (Eph. 4:1) and not follow the practices of the unsaved world (v. 17). This means living in love (5:2), in wisdom (v. 15), and in the Spirit (v. 18). To do anything less is to live beneath our high calling and the privileges we have as the children of God.

E–25

Immature Christians want the Lord to give them rules and regulations to cover every area of life, and this explains why they're immature. If we never have to pray, search the Scriptures, counsel with other believers, and wait on the Lord, we never will use our "spiritual muscles" and grow up. The Bible gives us precepts, principles, promises, and personal examples that together are adequate to guide us in the decisions of life. The

35

motor club will give its members detailed maps for their trips, but the Bible is more of a compass that keeps us going in the right direction without spelling out every detail of the trip. "For we walk by faith, not by sight" (2 Cor. 5:7).

J–118–19

As children of God, we already have everything we need for "life and godliness" (2 Peter 1:3), because we now possess "every spiritual blessing in Christ" (Eph. 1:3 NIV). But to possess these blessings is one thing; to enjoy them is quite something else. As we trust God's promises and obey His commandments, we draw upon our spiritual inheritance and are able to walk successfully and serve effectively. Like the nation of Israel in Canaan, we have battles to fight and work to do; but as we walk in obedience to the Lord, He enables us to overcome the enemy, claim the land, and enjoy its blessings.

J–137

The believer who truly knows and loves the Lord does not have to work at making his Christian life evident to others. In fact, he *shouldn't* have to work at it. His love for Christ should be obvious in what he says and does. Just as two people in love desire to talk about each other, our love for Christ should also compel us to tell others about Him.

NN–77

The Christian life is not easy, but we make it much more difficult by insisting on explanations. God's ways are above our ways; and even if He did explain His ways to us, would that heal our broken hearts? Probably not. Our hearts begin to heal, not when we can explain God's ways but when we trust God's Word and draw upon His unfailing grace.

AA–21

"Neither count I my life dear unto myself. . . ." There is a principle in the spiritual life that says: whatever you keep, you lose; whatever you give, you possess forever. If you count your life dear to yourself, and protect your own interests, and pamper yourself, then you will never really live. But if you yield yourself to the Lord and let Him control your life, you will enjoy abundant life.

TT–55

As Christians, we must live a day at a time. No person, no matter how wealthy or gifted, can live two days at a time. God provides for us "day by day" as we pray to Him (Luke 11:3). He gives us the strength that we need according to our daily requirements (Deut. 33:25). We must not make the mistake of trying to "store up grace" for future emergencies, because God gives us the grace that we need when we need it (Heb. 4:16). When we learn to live a day at a time, confident of God's care, it takes a great deal of pressure off of our lives.

Yard by yard, life is hard!

Inch by inch, life's a cinch!

RR–644

The Christian life is "a land of hills and valleys" (Deut. 11:11). In one day, a disciple can move from the glory of heaven to the attacks of hell.

RR–141

Christlikeness

The fact that we shall one day see Christ and be like Him should motivate us to live like Christ today.

SS–16

Church

When the church is least like the world, it does the most for the world.

SS–23

What every church should be is what every Christian should be:

elect (born again), *exemplary* (imitating the right people), *enthusiastic* (sharing the gospel with others), and *expectant* (daily looking for Jesus Christ to return).

SS–163

I'd rather be a struggling Christian in an imperfect church than a perfect sinner outside the church. One of the church fathers said that the church was something like Noah's ark: if it weren't for the judgment on the outside, you could never stand the smell on the inside.

WW–11

Renewal? Perhaps in some ministries; but for the most part, it's "business as usual." It will take more to move the church than rearranging the worship service and hanging up a few banners.

Reassessment? Yes, a lot of studies are going on, and we hope they will be useful. But I fear that the church body is getting an autopsy at a time when it really needs a resurrection.

WW–15

We are more like a defeated army, naked before our enemies, and unable to fight back because they have made a frightening discovery: the church is lacking in integrity.

WW–17

When the church, trying to reach the world, became like the world, she lost her impact on the world. How tragic that we cooperated with the enemy in *breaking down our own walls!* We lost our own distinctiveness and destroyed our own defenses.

WW–81

The church needs people who are doers of the Word and not just hearers, because the crisis won't be solved by spectators and armchair generals. God pity us! We preach unity and continue to "do our own thing," even if doing it hurts the work of others. We preach separation from the world and practice compromise. We preach love and then secretly rejoice when a brother or sister falls. We're so tolerant of sin in our own lives and in the lives of others that we don't dare get too specific in our preaching.

We need revival.

WW–131

Circumstances

When you find yourself in difficult circumstances because of God's discipline or because of someone else's disobedience, you can make one of three decisions. You can decide to *cover up,* which is what Naomi did; you can decide to *give up,* which is what Orpah did; or you can decide to *stand up* and believe God, which is what Ruth did.

LL–23

Before God changes our circumstances, He wants to change our hearts. If our circumstances change for the better, but we remain the same, then we will become worse. God's purpose in providence is not to make us comfortable, but to make us conformable, "conformed to the image of His Son" (Rom. 8:29 NASB). Christlike character is the divine goal for each of His children.

D–27

God alone is in control of circumstances. You are safer in a famine *in His will* than in a palace *out of His will.* It has well been said, "The will of God will never lead you where the grace of God cannot keep you." Abraham failed the test of circumstances and turned from the will of God.

L–23

No matter what our circumstances may be, we can trust God to be faithful. "Great is Thy faithfulness" isn't just a verse to quote (Lam. 3:23) or a song to sing. It's a glorious truth to believe and to act upon, no matter how difficult the situation in life might be.

38

"I will sing of the mercies of the Lord forever; with my mouth I will make known Your faithfulness to all generations" (Ps. 89:1 NKJV).

I–34

Someone has defined "circumstances" as "those nasty things you see when you get your eyes off of God." If you look at God through your circumstances, He will seem small and very far away; but if by faith you look at your circumstances through God, He will draw very near and reveal His greatness to you.

C–111

Comfort

The comfort of God comes to those who trust the grace of God, not to those who try to earn God's comfort by unnatural sorrow. Even though our sorrows may be caused by our sins, as were David's, we can still confess those sins to the Lord, claim His forgiveness, and experience His comfort.

DD–61

Commandments

It has often been said that "God's commandments are God's enablements." Once God has called and commissioned us, all we have to do is obey Him by faith, and He will do the rest. God cannot lie and God never fails. Faith means obeying God in spite of what we see, how we feel, or what the consequences might be. Our modern "practical" world laughs at faith without realizing that people live by faith all day long. "If there was no faith, there would be no living in this world," wrote humorist John Billings nearly a century ago. "We couldn't even eat hash with safety."

B–50

Communion

Paul did not say that we had to be *worthy* to partake of the Supper, but only that we should partake *in a worthy manner.*

If we are to participate in a worthy manner, we must examine our own hearts, judge our sins, and confess them to the Lord. To come to the table with unconfessed sin in our lives is to be guilty of Christ's body and blood, for it was sin that nailed Him to the cross. If we will not judge our own sins, then God will judge us and chasten us until we do confess and forsake our sins.

RR–606

Companionship

Companionship must be cultivated. Our Lord does not want to

be a divine lifeguard who is summoned only in emergencies. He wants to be involved in every aspect of our lives.

Y–74

Compassion

While believers must not compromise with the unsaved in matters of spiritual walk and ministry (2 Cor. 6:14–7:1), they may cooperate when it comes to caring for humanity and "promoting the general welfare." When you see that people are in trouble, you don't ask them for a testimony before helping them (Luke 10:25–37; Gal. 6:10). Sacrificial service is one way of showing the love of Christ to others (Matt. 5:16). If Christians don't carry their share of the common burdens of life, how can they be the salt of the earth and the light of the world?

L–33–34

One evidence of our Lord's compassion was the way He identified with outcasts. He ate with publicans and sinners (Matt. 9:9–13), touched the lepers (Matt. 8:1–4), accepted gifts from prostitutes (Luke 7:36–50), and even died between two criminals (23:32–33). Jesus knew what it was like to be "despised and rejected of men, a man of sorrows, and acquainted with grief" (Isa. 53:3). How important it is that we, His disciples, have this same kind of compassion. It's easy to identify with people we know and like when they are going through trials, but we tend to overlook the helpless, the poor, and the neglected in their sufferings.

M–73

Complacency

Complacency is an insidious sin, because it's based on lies, motivated by pride, and leads to trusting something other than God (Zeph. 1:12). Like the people in the church of Laodicea, complacent people consider themselves "rich, and increased with goods" and in need of nothing (Rev. 3:17). In reality, however, they have lost everything that's important in the spiritual life. When the Lord sees His people becoming complacent and self-satisfied, He sometimes sends trials to wake them up.

E–57

Confession

What is "confession of sin"? It is much more than simply admitting we have sinned. The Hebrew word means "to acknowledge," while the Greek word (as in 1 John 1:9) means "to say the same thing." These two ideas are joined in Psalm 51:3–4.

True confession of sin is not just with the lips, for there must also be a broken heart (Ps. 51:16–17) and a surrendered will. When we confess our sins, we acknowledge that what God says about them is true. We also *judge* our sins (1 Cor. 11:31) and turn from them. What many people think is confession of sin is really only *excusing* sin and looking for a way to escape from the consequences!

GG–58

Conformable

In one of my radio messages, I made the statement, "God does not expect us to be comfortable, but He does expect us to be conformable." No sooner had the program ended than my office phone rang and an anonymous listener wanted to argue with me about that statement.

"Conformable to what?" the voice thundered. "Haven't you read Romans 12:2—'Be not conformed to this world'?"

"Sure I've read Romans 12:2," I replied. "Have you read Romans 8:29? God has predestined us 'to be conformed to the image of His Son.'"

After a long pause (I was glad he was paying the phone bill), he grunted and said, "OK."

Comfortable or *conformable:* that is the question. If we are looking for comfortable lives, then we will protect our plans and desires, save our lives, and never be planted. But if we yield our lives and let God plant us, we will never be alone but will have the joy of being fruitful to the glory of God. "If any man [Jew or Greek] serve Me, let him follow Me." This is the equivalent of Matthew 10:39 and Mark 8:36.

RR–342

Conscience

Our spiritual senses function in a similar way. If we don't exercise our spiritual senses, then we never learn how to discern between good and evil, and then we don't grow in Christian character. It is important for us to build up our conscience—to have a good conscience, a pure conscience, a conscience void of offense—because this helps us to build Christian character.

FF–22

Jesus said conscience is like your eye. The eye does not manufacture light—the eye lets light in. When the light comes into our lives, it gives us guidance. But suppose that every time we do something wrong, the window gets dirtier until finally we have sinned so

41

much that the window is completely covered with dirt. The light cannot come through, and so we are left in the darkness!

FF–11

We learned from Hebrews 8 that the ministry of the New Covenant is *internal.* "I will put My laws into their mind, and write them in their hearts" (Heb. 8:10). This work is done by the Holy Spirit of God (2 Cor. 3:1–3). But the Spirit could not dwell within us if Jesus Christ had not paid for our sins. Cleansing our consciences cannot be done by some external ceremony; it demands an internal power. Because Jesus Christ is "without spot [blemish]" He was able to offer the perfect sacrifice.

SS–311

Our English word *conscience* comes from two Latin words: *com,* meaning "with," and *scire,* meaning "to know." Conscience is that inner faculty that "knows with" our spirit and approves when we do right, but accuses when we do wrong. Conscience is not the Law of God, but it bears witness to that Law. It is the window that lets in the light; and if the window gets dirty because we disobey, then the light becomes dimmer and dimmer (see Matt. 6:22–23; Rom. 2:14–16).

Paul used the word *conscience* twenty-three times in his letters and spoken ministry as given in Acts. "And herein do I exercise myself, to have always a conscience void of offense toward God, and toward men" (Acts 24:16). When a person has a good conscience, he has integrity, not duplicity; and he can be trusted.

RR–632

You cannot glorify Christ and practice deception at the same time. If you do, you will violate your conscience and erode your character; but eventually the truth will come out.

RR–633–34

Contemporary

I think we have confused novelty and change and have hidden this confusion under the guise of being contemporary. Change for the sake of change is simply novelty, and it does not last. Change for the sake of improvement is progress, and progress is what we need. The sad thing about the contemporary emphasis is that it may keep us from diagnosing the real sickness in the church and securing the remedy. We are rearranging the furniture while the walls are falling down.

W–35

The church must always minister to present generations. In order to do this well, it must understand what people are thinking, what they are seeking, and what authority they are respecting. But this does not mean we must become like the secular world in order to get a hearing. Identification with the world and its needs is one thing; imitation of the world and its foolishness is quite another.

W–35

Contentment

True contentment comes from godliness in the heart, not wealth in the hand. A person who depends on material things for peace and assurance will never be satisfied, for material things have a way of losing their appeal. It is the wealthy people, not the poor people, who go to psychiatrists and who are more apt to try to commit suicide.

SS–235

Contentment cannot come from material things, for they can never satisfy the heart. Only God can do that. "Watch out! Be on your guard against all kinds of greed; a man's life does not consist in the abundance of his possessions" (Luke 12:15 NIV). When we have God, we have all that we need. The material things of life can decay or be stolen, but *God* will never leave us or forsake us.

SS–327

Contentment is not escape from the battle, but rather an abiding peace and confidence in the midst of the battle. "I have learned, in whatsoever state I am, therewith to be content" (Phil. 4:11). Two words in that verse are vitally important— "learned" and "content."

SS–97

Conviction

There must be conviction before a sinner can experience conversion. Unless a patient is convinced that he is sick, he will never accept the diagnosis or take the treatment.

RR–413

Counselor

Where people turn for help is some indication of their character and faith. One man turns to the local bar where he pours out his troubles into the ears of anybody he thinks will be sympathetic. (But then he has to listen to their troubles!) Others visit "readers" or fortune-tellers, or perhaps pay to have their horoscope cast. Many people talk their problems over with a doctor or a pastor, or perhaps visit a psychologist or other trained counselor.

To the Christian, Jesus Christ is the supreme Counselor. "Lord, to whom shall we go? You have the words of eternal life" (John 6:68 NIV). While it's helpful to talk to friends and professional counselors, our first obligation is to talk to the Lord and listen to His Word. The fact that He is called "Counselor" reveals several important truths to us that help us in making the decisions of life.

ZZ–28

Counterfeit

We must beware of Satan's counterfeits. He has counterfeit Christians (2 Cor. 11:26) who believe a counterfeit gospel (Gal. 1:6–9). He encourages a counterfeit righteousness (Rom. 10:1–3), and even has a counterfeit church (Rev. 2:9). At the end of the age, Satan will produce a counterfeit Christ (2 Thess. 2:1–12).

RR–45

Covenant, Old, New

We must not conclude that the existence of the New Covenant means that the Old Covenant was wrong or that the Law has no ministry today. Both covenants were given by God. Both covenants were given for people's good. Both covenants had blessings attached to them. If Israel had obeyed the terms of the Old Covenant, God would have blessed them and they would have been ready for the coming of their Messiah. Paul pointed out that the Old Covenant had its share of glory (2 Cor. 3:7–11). We must not criticize the Old Covenant or minimize it.

SS–306

Yes, our Lord *is* ministering on the basis of a better covenant, a New Covenant that makes us partakers of the new nature and the wonderful new life that only Christ can give.

SS–308

The only "eternal covenant" that has lasted—and that will last—is the one made by the eternal God, sealed by the blood of Jesus Christ.

SS–22

Covetousness

The word *covetousness* literally means "love of money"; but it can be applied to a love for *more* of anything. Someone asked millionaire Bernard Baruch, "How much money does it take for a rich man to be satisfied?" Baruch replied, "Just a million more than he has." Covetousness is the desire for more, whether we need it or not.

SS–327

Creation

When it comes to Creation, Jesus Christ is the primary cause (He planned it), the instrumental cause (He produced it), and the final cause (He did it for His own pleasure).

SS–116

Criticism

One pastor had a sign on his desk that read LOOK BEYOND THE CRITIC. It reminded him to see the Lord on the throne, to see the total church ministry and the many friends who loved him, and to see the purposes God wanted to achieve.

Z–19

President Harry Truman used to say to his colleagues, "If you can't take the heat, get out of the kitchen!" We may not like it, but criticism is a part of the ministry; and the pastor with a thin skin or a sensitive ego has to learn how to take it.

Z–27

Cross

The cross was a divine assignment, not a human accident; it was a God-given obligation, not human option.

UU–12

By His death on the cross, Jesus fulfilled the entire sacrificial system and put an end to it forever. He accomplished with one offering what millions of animals on Jewish altars could never accomplish, "for it is not possible that the blood of bulls and goats could take away sins" (Heb. 10:4 NKJV).

UU–13

The battle Jesus fought on the cross against the powers of hell wasn't a minor skirmish; it was a major assault that ended in a complete victory for the Savior.

UU–32

Religion that rejects the cross is both impotent and ignorant, for the Christ of the cross is "the power of God and the wisdom of God" (1 Cor. 1:24). Only the Christ of the cross can bring us to God. Respectable religion that rejects the blood of the cross can't understand the message of the Bible, and it is powerless to deal with sin and sinful human nature. "Comfortable religion" that avoids bearing the cross and following Jesus is but a religious facade that knows nothing of true discipleship.

UU–42

45

D

Darkness

At times God permits His children to experience darkness on a dead-end street where they don't know which way to turn. When this happens, *wait for the Lord to give you light in His own time.* Don't try to manufacture your own light or to borrow light from others. Follow the wise counsel of Isaiah, "Who among you fears the LORD? Who obeys the voice of His Servant? Who walks in darkness and has no light? Let him trust in the name of the LORD and rely upon his God" (Isa. 50:10 NKJV).

M–71–72

Deacon

A deacon who does not *know* the Word of God cannot manage the affairs of the church of God. A deacon who does not *live* the Word of God, but has a "defiled conscience," cannot manage the church of God. Simply because a church member is popular, successful in business, or generous in his giving does not mean he is qualified to serve as a deacon.

SS–222

The great doctrines of the faith are hidden to those outside the faith, but they can be understood by those who trust the Lord. Deacons must understand Christian doctrine and obey it with a good conscience. It is not enough to sit in meetings and decide how to "run the church." They must base their decisions on the Word of God, and they must back up their decisions with godly lives.

SS–222

Death

Sigmund Freud, the founder of psychiatry, wrote: "And finally there is the painful riddle of death, for which no remedy at all has yet been found, nor probably ever will be." Christians have victory *in* death and *over* death! Why? Because of the victory of Jesus Christ in His own resurrection. Jesus said, "Because I live, ye shall also" (John 14:19).

Sin, death, and the Law go together. The Law reveals sin, and the "wages of sin is death" (Rom. 6:23). Jesus bore our sins on the cross (1 Peter 2:24), and also bore the curse of the Law (Gal. 3:13). It is through Him that we have this victory, and we share the victory *today*. The literal translation of 1 Corinthians 15:57 is, "But thanks be to God who *keeps on giving us the victory* through our Lord Jesus Christ." We experience "the power of His resurrection" in our lives as we yield to Him (Phil. 3:10 NASB).

RR–619

In what sense did Satan have the power of death? The final authority of death is in the hands of our God (Deut. 32:39; Matt. 10:28; Rev. 1:18). Satan can do only that which is permitted by God (Job 1:12; 2:6). But because Satan is the author of sin (John 8:44), and sin brings death (Rom. 6:23), in this sense Satan exercises power in the realm of death. Jesus called him a murderer (John 8:44). Satan uses the fear of death as a terrible weapon to gain control over the lives of people. His kingdom is one of darkness and death (Col. 1:13). We who

trust in Jesus Christ have once and for all been delivered from Satan's authority and from the terrible fear of death. The death, burial, and resurrection of Christ have given us victory (1 Cor. 15:55–58)!

SS–284

Decisions

There is no need to fear the decisions of life when you know Jesus Christ, for His name is Counselor.

Y–41

The decisions made today in the high places of government and finance seem remote from the everyday lives of God's people, but they affect us and God's work in many ways. It's good to know that God is on His throne and that no decision is made that can thwart His purposes. "He does as he pleases with the powers of heaven and the peoples of the earth. No one can hold back his hand or say to him: 'What have you done?'" (Dan. 4:35 NIV).

"There is no attribute of God more comforting to His children than the doctrine of divine sovereignty," said Charles Haddon Spurgeon. While we confess that many things involved in this doctrine are shrouded in mystery, it's unthinkable that Almighty God should not be Master of His own universe.

Even in the affairs of a pagan empire, God is in control.

D–85

Desires

God has given man certain desires, and these desires are good. Hunger, thirst, weariness, and sex are not at all evil in themselves. There is nothing wrong about eating, drinking, sleeping, or begetting children. But when the flesh nature controls them, they become sinful "lusts." Hunger is not evil, but gluttony is sinful. Thirst is not evil, but drunkenness is a sin. Sleep is a gift of God, but laziness is shameful. Sex is God's precious gift when used rightly; but when used wrongly, it becomes immorality.

S–492

Diligence

"Give diligence" is a good translation of this admonition, "Let us labor" (Heb. 4:9–13). Diligence is the opposite of "drifting" (Heb. 2:1–3). How do we give diligence? By paying close attention to the Word of God. Israel did not believe God's Word, so the rebels fell in the wilderness. "So then faith cometh by hearing, and hearing by the Word of God" (Rom. 10:17).

SS–289

Disappointments

God builds character in the disappointments of life and He also gives a witness. In the midst of his disappointments, Jeremiah bore witness to the Lord and gave His message to the people. By his preaching and his living, Jeremiah pointed others to God. Disappointments are not only opportunities for maturity, but they are also opportunities for ministry. We today have the writings of Jeremiah for our own learning and living because the prophet was faithful to God. When you accept disappointments, trust God, and yield to Him, you leave something behind to help others in the battles of life.

TT–45

Disciple, Discipleship

Effective discipleship depends on close attention to the Word of God. The Spirit of God teaches us from the Word, and then He directs our lives into circumstances that force us to trust the Word and act upon it. It has well been said that life is a school in which you learn what the lessons were *after* you take the test. Jesus taught His disciples and then sent them out to serve. They would come back, report on their ministry, and then learn again the lessons they had forgotten. It was only after they had proved what they had learned that Jesus would impart new truths to them.

XX–64–65

We are not saved from our sins because we take up a cross and follow Jesus, but because we trust the Savior who died on the cross for our sins. After we become children of God, then we become disciples.

The closest contemporary word to "disciple" is probably "apprentice." A disciple is more than a student who learns lessons by means of lectures and books. He is one who learns by living and working with his teacher in a daily "hands on" experience. Too many Christians are content to be listeners who gain a lot of knowledge but who have never put that knowledge into practice.

RR–207

Discipleship is a daily discipline: we follow Jesus a step at a time, a day at a time. A weary cleaning woman said to a friend of mine, "The trouble with life is that it's so daily!" But she was wrong. One of the *best* things about life is that we can take it a day at a time (Deut. 33:25).

RR–207

Discipline

What a tragedy when children are left to themselves, not knowing where or what the boundaries are and what the consequences of rebellion will be! I may be wrong, but I have a suspicion that many people who can't discipline their children have a hard time disciplining themselves. If you want to enjoy your children all your life, start by lovingly disciplining them early. "The rod and rebuke give wisdom, but a child left to himself brings shame to his mother" (Prov. 29:15 NKJV).

O–105

If our churches do not deal with sin, the sin will grow and will infect other people. Before long you will have a real problem on your hands. Church discipline is not a policeman's finding a culprit and throwing him in jail. Church discipline is a brokenhearted shepherd's finding a wayward sheep, weeping, praying, and trying to restore him.

H–34

Discipline is to the believer what exercise and training are to the athlete (Heb. 12:11); it enables us to run the race with endurance and reach the assigned goal (vv. 1–2).

A–78

Discouragement

As by faith we claim our inheritance in Christ, we experience peaks of victory and valleys of discouragement. Discouragement isn't inevitable in the Christian life, but we must remember that we can't have mountains without valleys.

P–83

We need to remember that the God we serve is all-powerful. He is greater than any problem we may have. He is greater than our enemies: "Greater is he that is in you, than he that is in the world" (1 John 4:4). If you are feeling discouraged and defeated, perhaps you need to be reminded once again of all that the Lord has done for you. When you pause to reflect on these blessings, then you can say with Fanny Crosby, "To God be the glory— great things He hath done!"

NN–48

Disobedience

There are three forces that encourage man in his disobedience—the world, the devil, and the flesh.

SS–18

Never underestimate the amount of damage one person can do outside the will of God. Abraham's disobedience in Egypt almost cost him his wife (Gen. 12:10–20); David's disobedience in taking an unauthorized census led to the death of 70,000 people (2 Sam. 24); and Jonah's refusal to obey God almost sank a ship (Jonah 1). The church today must look diligently "lest any root of bitterness springing up cause trouble" (Heb. 12:15 NKJV). That's why Paul admonished the Corinthian believers to discipline the disobedient man in their fellowship, because his sin was defiling the whole church (1 Cor. 5).

P–84

Dissension

Whenever you find division and dissension in a local church, it is usually because of selfishness and sin on the part of the leaders, or the members, or both. James 4:1–3 makes it clear that selfishness on the inside leads to strife on the outside. It is only as we submit to one another in the Lord that we can enjoy His blessing, and peace in the family.

SS–187

Doctrine

When a person does not know the doctrines of the Christian faith, he can easily be captured by false religions.

SS–125

50

It is one thing for us to defend a doctrine in a church meeting, and quite something else to put it into practice in everyday life.

RR–694

Doubt

"Men of faith are always the men who have to confront problems," wrote G. Campbell Morgan, for if you believe in God, you sometimes wonder why He allows certain things to happen. But keep in mind that there's a difference between doubt and unbelief. Like Habakkuk, the doubter questions God and may even debate with God, but the doubter doesn't abandon God. But unbelief is rebellion against God, a refusal to accept what He says and does. Unbelief is an act of the will, while doubt is born out of a troubled mind and a broken heart.

A–109

It is not unusual for great spiritual leaders to have their days of doubt and uncertainty. Moses was ready to quit on one occasion (Num. 11:10–15), and so were Elijah (1 Kings 19) and Jeremiah (Jer. 20:7–9, 14–18); and even Paul knew the meaning of despair (2 Cor. 1:8–9).

There is a difference between doubt and unbelief. Doubt is a matter of the mind: we cannot understand what God is doing or why He is doing it. Unbelief is a matter of the will: we refuse to believe God's Word and obey what He tells us to do. "Doubt is not always a sign that a man is wrong," said Oswald Chambers; "it may be a sign that he is thinking."

RR–196–97

Duty

As His servants, we must beware lest we have the wrong attitude toward our duties. There are two extremes to avoid: merely doing our duty in a slavish way *because we have to,* or doing our duty *because we hope to gain a reward.* Christian industrialist R. G. LeTourneau used to say, "If you give because it pays, *it won't pay.*" This principle also applies to service. Both extremes are seen in the attitudes of the elder brother (Luke 15:25–32) who was miserably obedient, always hoping that his father would let him have a party with his friends.

RR–244

E

Elect, Election

A local church must be composed of elect people, those who have been saved by the grace of God. One problem today is the presence, in the church family, of unbelievers whose names may be on the church roll, but not written in the Lamb's Book of Life. Every church member should examine his heart to determine whether he has truly been born again and belongs to God's elect.

SS–162

The fact that we are God's elect people does not excuse us from the task of evangelism. On the contrary, the doctrine of election is one of the greatest encouragements to evangelism.

SS–162

The same God who ordained the end (salvation) also ordained the means to the end ("belief of the truth"). The person who says, "God already has His elect, so there is no need for us to pray, witness, and send out missionaries" does not understand divine election. The greatest encouragement to evangelism is the knowledge that God has His people who have been prepared to respond to His Word (read Acts 18:1–11).

In order for God to fulfill His eternal plan, He sent Paul, Silas, and Timothy to Thessalonica to preach the Word of God. What was ordained *in eternity* was accomplished *in time.* God used human instruments to bring the gospel to the lost; and by trusting Christ, these people proved their "election of God" (1 Thess. 1:4). The call of God went out to the whole city, but it was effective only in those who believed the truth and trusted Christ.

SS–201

"Am I one of God's elect?" is not the question the lost sinner should

52

ask. The admonition to "make your calling and election sure" was written to believers (2 Peter 1:10), not to lost sinners. The question the lost sinner should ask is, "What must I do to be saved?" (Acts 16:30; cf. 2:37). And the answer is, "Believe on the Lord Jesus Christ" (16:31). When God is speaking to you, that is the time to respond and put your faith in Christ (Isa. 55:6–7).

L–124

Two lines of truth seem to run parallel in the Bible: one, that God has chosen His "elect" from eternity, and two, that these "elect" have made a responsible decision to trust Christ. "All that the Father gives Me will come to Me [that's divine election], and the one who comes to Me [that's human responsibility] I will by no means cast out" (John 6:37 NASB). If we deny divine election, then we make salvation the work of man. If we deny human responsibility, then we make man *less than* man, a mere robot fulfilling the eternal plan of God. "Salvation is of the LORD" (Jonah 2:9) expresses divine sovereignty. "Seek the LORD while He may be found" (Isa. 55:6 NASB) expresses human responsibility.

A paradox? Yes. A mystery? To be sure! An impossibility? No! One of my professors at seminary said, "Try to explain divine election,

and you may lose your mind. Try to explain it away, and you may lose your soul." Truth is not always at one extreme or the other. Sometimes truth is found at that subtle point of paradox where two opposites meet. At any rate, it is not necessary for a lost sinner to comprehend the mysteries of divine election in order to be saved. He knows that God loves him (John 3:16) and that God is not willing that any should perish (1 Peter 3:9). He knows that the promise of salvation is for "everyone who calls on the name of the Lord" (Acts 2:21 NIV). If he calls, God will answer him and save him.

H–36

A review of 2 Thessalonians 2:13–14 shows that all three persons in the Trinity are involved in our calling. God the Father chose us, God the Son died for us, and God the Spirit convicted us and imparted new life when we trusted Christ. Before I was saved, I knew nothing about divine election. But after I became a Christian and started reading my Bible, I discovered to my amazement that God in His grace had chosen me long before I even knew Him!

The beloved former pastor of the Moody Church in Chicago, Dr. Harry Ironside, used to illustrate this truth by describing a door. The sinner is standing outside the door and he reads above it, "Whosoever will, let him come!" He believes God's promise, steps through the door, and is saved. He then turns around and reads above the *inside* of the door, "Chosen in Christ before the foundation of the world."

Q–41

Encouragement

Nehemiah didn't pay much attention to complainers but went right on with the work. That's the best thing to do. If you take time away from your work to listen to everybody who wants your attention, you will never get anything done. Nehemiah got his encouragement from prayer and the promises of God, and the occasional complaints of some of the people didn't upset him.

D–55

Enemies, Spiritual

In John 14:30–31, the Lord named two of our great spiritual enemies—the world and the devil. Jesus overcame the world and the devil (John 12:31), and the devil has no claim on Him. There is no point in Jesus Christ where the devil can get a foothold. Since we are "in Christ," Satan can get no foothold in the believer's life, unless we per-

mit it. Neither Satan nor the world can trouble our hearts if we are yielded to the "peace of God" through the Holy Spirit.

RR–354

We have three spiritual enemies—the world, the flesh, and the devil. Paul made it clear in Ephesians 6:12 that our problem is not people: "We wrestle not against flesh and blood." When strife and problems exist, our trouble is not with the person but with Satan, who is working in and through that person. Satan can even use a believer. He used Peter. When the apostle was trying to divert Jesus from His plan for mankind, Jesus said to Peter, "Get thee behind me, Satan" (Matt. 16:23). The devil used Ananias and Sapphira, filling them with greed and lies (see Acts 5:1–11). The Enemy loves to control us, causing us to do and say things we shouldn't.

GGG–13

Eternal Life, Eternal, Eternity

As the eternal Holy Spirit works in our lives, we participate in the eternal plan and work of God. As we obey His Word, our lives take on the quality of the eternal. We live *in* time, but we live *for* eternity. "He that doeth the will of God abideth forever" (1 John 2:17).

Y–66

The eternal is so glorious that the temporal with its burdens and problems does not defeat us. The outward man is perishing, but the inward man is being renewed day by day.

Y–66

When Jesus Christ is in control of your life, each moment is an eternal experience because He gives to you a quality of life that comes out of eternity. "Eternal life" means much more than living forever, for even the lost are going to exist forever. "Eternal life" means "the life of eternity." It is an experience in Christ here and now!

Y–65

People have the mistaken idea that "eternal life" is simply endless time, an unlimited quantity of years. Eternal life is beyond time; it is the very life of God in the believer *today*. When you trust Jesus Christ, you receive eternal life; so that, for you, heaven has already begun within your own heart. You are living "in time" but enjoying eternity!

GG–40

Consider the characteristics of this gift of eternal life. Certainly it is the most *expensive* gift ever given, for it cost Jesus Christ His life. It is an *eternal* gift. Unlike most of the gifts we receive, which either break or wear out, eternal life gets better and better as the years move on. Eternal life is an *essential* gift—everybody needs it. If you had to give one gift to everybody in the world, what would it be? Not everyone can read books; not everyone wears the same kind of clothing; not everybody needs money; tastes in food differ from one place to another. The only gift that is suitable for everybody is eternal life, for everybody needs it.

H–40

Evangelism

Balanced evangelism presents to the sinner both repentance and faith.

RR–414

Examine

If the greatest sin is the corruption of the highest good, then Judah was guilty of great sin. Their highest good was to know the true God and worship Him, but they perverted that blessing and worshiped idols. They turned His temple into a den of thieves, persecuted His prophets, rejected His covenant, and disgraced His name. "God's name is blasphemed among the Gentiles because of

55

you" (Rom. 2:24 NIV; see Ezek. 36:22). God patiently dealt with His people, seeking to woo them back, but they only hardened their hearts and turned a deaf ear to His warnings.

Before we condemn the people of Judah, however, let's examine our own hearts and churches. Are there idols in our hearts? Do we give wholehearted devotion to the Lord, or is our devotion divided between Christ and another? When unsaved people visit our worship services, are they impressed with the glory and majesty of God (1 Cor. 14:23–25)? Do the worldly lives and questionable activities of professed believers disgrace God's name? Remember, God's "last word" to the church isn't the Great Commission; it's "Repent, or else!" (Rev. 2–3).

F–59

As God's church today faces enemies and challenges, it is always a temptation to turn to the world or the flesh for help. But our first response must be to examine our hearts to see if there is something we need to confess and make right. Then we must run to the Lord in faith and obedience and surrender to His will alone. We must trust Him to protect us and fight for us.

C–80

Exercise

Nourishment without exercise will make a person overweight, sluggish, and fair game for a variety of physical problems. What's true of the body is also true of the inner person: unless we devote ourselves to spiritual exercise, the nourishment we take will probably do us more harm than good. Too many saints are overfed and underexercised, and that's why Paul tied food and exercise together when he wrote these words to Timothy: "For bodily exercise profits a little, but godliness is profitable for all things, having promise of the life that now is and of that which is to come" (1 Tim. 4:8 NKJV).

K–69

F

Failure

No matter how badly we have failed, we can always get up and begin again; for our God is the God of new beginnings.

P–97

Each one of us, at one time or another, will fail the Lord as Peter did and then hear (in one way or another) "the crowing of the cock." Satan will tell us that we are finished, that our future has been destroyed, but that is not God's message to us. It was certainly not the end for Peter! His restoration was so complete that he was able to say to the Jews, "But you denied the Holy One and the Just!" (Acts 3:14 NKJV). Peter did not have 1 John 1:9 to read, but he did experience it in his own heart.

RR–271–72

Bible history is filled with people who began the race with great success but failed at the end because they disregarded God's rules. They did not lose their salvation, but they did lose their rewards (1 Cor. 3:15). It happened to Lot (Gen. 19), Samson (Judg. 16), Saul (1 Sam. 28:31), and Ananias and Sapphira (Acts 5). And it can happen to us! It is an exciting experience to run the race daily, "looking unto Jesus" (Heb. 12:1–2). It will be even more exciting when we experience that "upward calling" and Jesus returns to take us to heaven! Then we will stand before the *bema* to receive our rewards! It was this future prospect that motivated Paul, and it can also motivate us.

SS–91

Faith

It takes faith to obey God, but God always rewards obedient faith.

Y–98

57

A lady was arguing with her pastor about this matter of faith and works. "I think that getting to heaven is like rowing a boat," she said. "One oar is faith, and the other is works. If you use both, you get there. If you use only one, you go around in circles."

"There is only one thing wrong with your illustration," replied the pastor. "Nobody is going to heaven *in a rowboat!*"

There is only one "good work" that takes the sinner to heaven: the finished work of Christ on the cross (John 17:1–4; 19:30; Heb. 10:11–14).

SS–85

Saving faith involves the mind, the emotions, and the will. With the mind we understand the truth of the gospel, and with the heart we feel conviction and the need to be saved. But it is only when we exercise the will and commit ourselves to Christ that the process is complete. Faith is not mental assent to a body of doctrines, no matter how true those doctrines may be. Faith is not emotional concern. *Faith is commitment to Jesus Christ.*

SS–107

What is the relationship between faith, hope, and love? Certainly the more we love someone, the more we will trust him. We do not trust a casual acquaintance to the same degree that we trust a confidential friend. As we come to know God better, we trust Him more and we love Him more. Love and faith encourage each other.

SS–109

If you want to claim your spiritual inheritance in Christ, believe the Word of faith and *get your feet wet!* Step out in a walk of faith, and God will open the way for you. Surrender yourself to the Lord and die to the old life (Rom. 6), and He will bring you into the land and give you "days of heaven upon the earth" (Deut. 11:21).

P–55

God sometimes permits us to experience humiliating defeats in order to test our faith and reveal to us what's really going on in our hearts. What life does *to* us depends on what life finds *in* us, and we don't always know the condition of our own hearts (Jer. 17:9).

P–89

Faith means we trust His timing, we claim His promises, we rest in His love. Faith knows that He is the Master of every situation and that He is able even to conquer death.

AA–23

Faith, hope, and love: These are the great Christian virtues that should characterize all believers. Faith looks up to a God who can be trusted. Hope looks ahead to a future that is bright with the glory of God. And, lest we grow selfish, love looks around and shares God's blessing with others. All of this begins at the feet of Jesus.

AA–58

By faith, take off the graveclothes and bury the past. Leave it all in the tomb, and step out by faith into the wonderful freedom you have in Christ. This does not mean that God will obliterate the past, because He does want us to remember how He has led us and helped us (Deut. 8:2). Rather, it means that you will be able to look at the past without fear and regret; you will be free from bondage to the past.

AA–77

It's one thing to "whistle in the dark" and try to bolster our courage, and quite something else to sing about the eternal God who never fails.

A–135

God doesn't always change the circumstances, but He can change us to meet the circumstances. That's what it means to live by faith.

A–136

True Bible faith is confident obedience to God's Word in spite of cir- *cumstances and consequences.* This faith operates quite simply. God speaks and we hear His Word. We trust His Word and act on it no matter what the circumstances are or what the consequences may be. The circumstances may be impossible, and the consequences frightening and unknown; but we obey God's Word just the same and believe Him to do what is right and what is best.

The unsaved world does not understand true Bible faith, probably because it sees so little faith in action in the church today. The cynical editor H. L. Mencken defined faith as "illogical belief in the occurrence of the impossible." The world fails to realize that faith is only as good as its object, and the object of our faith is *God*. Faith is not some "feeling" that we manufacture. It is our total response to what God has revealed in His Word.

SS–317

According to the Bible, true faith is *obeying God in spite of feelings, circumstances, or consequences.* All of the men and women whose names are listed in "The Hall of Fame of Faith" had to deal with their emotions (did you ever walk through a sea?), their circumstances (did you ever fight an army?), and the consequences of their decisions (did you ever say no to a powerful ruler?). They did not deny their feelings; they could not change their circumstances; they could not predict the consequences. *But they trusted God,* and He saw them through.

MM–13

"Faith in faith" is not the same as faith in God, because it has no foundation. It is building on the sand (Matt. 7:24–27). *True faith is our obedient response to the Word of God.* God speaks, we hear Him and believe, and we do what He tells us to do. Abraham and Sarah held on to God's promises and God rewarded their faith.

L–136

How do you walk by faith? By claiming the promises of God and obeying the Word of God, in spite of what you see, how you feel, or what may happen. It means committing yourself to the Lord and relying wholly on Him to meet the need. When we live by faith, it glorifies God, witnesses to a lost world, and builds Christian character into our lives. God has ordained that "the righteous will live by his faith" (Hab. 2:4; Rom. 1:17; Gal. 3:11; Heb. 10:38; 2 Cor. 5:7 NIV); and when we refuse to trust Him, we are calling God a liar and dishonoring Him.

D–15–16

Faithfulness of God

Somehow we have the idea that when life is *easy,* God is with us; but when life is *hard,* God has forsaken us—and just the opposite might be true. Too often when life is easy we forget God and start to depend on our own wisdom and strength. It is when the going is hard that we really know how close God is to His needy children.

TT–27

False Teachers

It comes as a shock to some people that Satan uses professed Christians *in the church* to accomplish his work. But Satan once used Peter to try to lead Jesus on a wrong path (Matt. 16:21–23), and he used Ananias and Sapphira to try to deceive the church at Jerusalem (Acts 5). Paul warned that false teachers would arise *from within the church* (Acts 20:30).

Their goal is to seduce people and get them to depart from the faith. This is the word *apostasy,* and it is defined as "a willful turning away from the truth of the Christian faith." These false teachers do not try to build up the church or relate people to the Lord Jesus Christ in a deeper way. Instead they want to get disciples to follow them and join their groups and promote their programs. This is one difference between a true church and a religious cult: A true church seeks to win converts to Jesus Christ and to build them spiritually; conversely, a cult proselytizes, steals converts from others, and makes them servants (even slaves!) of the leaders of the cult. However, not all apostates are in cults; some of them are in churches *and pulpits,* teaching false doctrine and leading people astray.

These false teachers preach one thing but practice another. They tell their disciples what to do, but they do not do it themselves. Satan works "by means of the hypocrisy of liars" (1 Tim. 4:2, literal translation). One of the marks of a true servant of God is his honesty and integrity: He practices what he preaches.

SS–222

False teaching is like yeast: it enters secretly, it grows quickly, and permeates completely (Gal. 5:9). The best time to attack false doctrine is at the beginning, before it has a chance to spread.

The attitude of some church members is, "It makes no difference what you believe, just as long as you believe something." Paul would not agree with that foolish philosophy. It makes all the difference between life and death whether or not you believe the truth of the Word or believe lies. You can choose what you want to believe, but you cannot change the consequences.

SS–264

Fasting

True fasting will lead to humility before God and ministry to others. We deprive ourselves so that we might share with others and do so to the glory of God. If we fast in order to get something for ourselves from God, instead of to become better people for the sake of others, then we have missed the meaning of worship. It delights the Lord when we delight in the Lord.

C–152

Father

We do not have to wait until we enter heaven to get to know the Father. We can know Him today and receive from Him the spiritual resources we need to keep going when the days are difficult.

What does it mean to "know the Father"? The word *know* is used 141 times in John's Gospel, but it does not always carry the same meaning. In fact, there are four different "levels" of *knowing* according to John. The lowest level is simply knowing a fact. The next level is to understand the truth behind that fact. However, you can know the fact and know the truth behind it and still be lost in your sins. The third level introduces *relationship;* "to know" means "to believe in a person and become related to him or her." This is the way "know" is used in John 17:3.

RR–350

Four hundred years before Christ was born, the Greek philosopher Plato wrote, "To find out the Father and Maker of all this universe is a hard task, and when we have found Him, to speak of Him to all men is impossible." But Plato was wrong! We *can* know the Father and Maker of the universe, for Jesus Christ revealed Him to us. Why should our hearts be troubled when the Creator and Governor of the universe is *our own Father?*

The very Lord of heaven and earth is our Father (Luke 10:21). There is no need for us to have troubled hearts, for He is in control.

RR–351

The Old Testament Jew knew his God as "Jehovah," the great I AM (Exod. 3:11–14). Jesus took this sacred name "I AM" and made it meaningful to His disciples: "I am the bread of life" (John 6:35); "I am the light of the world" (John 8:12);

"I am the good shepherd" (John 10:11); etc. In other words, Jesus revealed the Father's gracious name by showing His disciples that He was everything they needed.

But the Father's name includes much more than this, for Jesus also taught His disciples that God—the great I AM—was their heavenly Father. The word *Father* is used 53 times in John 13–17, and 122 times in John's Gospel! In His messages to the Jews, Jesus made it clear that the Father sent Him, that He was equal to the Father, and that His words and works came from the Father. It was a clear claim to deity, but they refused to believe.

RR–368

Fear

Fear is a real problem today. Some people are afraid to go to the doctor because they fear that he will discover a serious problem. Other people do not read the newspaper or watch TV because they fear what is happening in the world. Many are afraid to "get involved" and help those in need because of their fear that the person will swindle or harm them. People are being shackled and paralyzed by their fear of the past, present, and future. They worry that the past will catch up with them, that they will not be able to cope with their present life, and that the future will hold even more problems for them. Yet time and time again God tells us in His Word, "Fear not, for I am with you."

NN–63

The foundation for Job's character was the fact that he "feared God and shunned evil." "Behold, the fear of the Lord, that is wisdom; and to depart from evil is understanding" (Job 28:28). To fear the Lord means to respect who He is, what He says, and what He does. It is not the cringing fear of a slave before a master but the loving reverence of a child before a father, a respect that leads to obedience. "The remarkable thing about fearing God," said Oswald Chambers, "is that when you fear God you fear nothing else, whereas if you do not fear God you fear everything else."

M–14

Fellowship

There is no substitute for daily fellowship with the Lord in His Word and in prayer, and then walking with Him in obedience.

Y–28

We have the fellowship of the church: "that they may be one, as we are" (John 17:11). The New Testament knows nothing of isolated believers; wherever you find saints you find them in fellowship. Why? Because God's people need each other. Jesus opened His Upper Room message by washing the disciples' feet and teaching them to minister to one another.

RR–369

Fishermen

True fishermen don't quit. Peter kept on working while Jesus used his ship as a platform from which to address the huge crowd on the shore. "Every pulpit is a fishing boat," said Dr. J. Vernon McGee, "a place to give out the Word of God and attempt to catch fish."

RR–185

Fools

Fools won't learn from God's Word. "The fear of the LORD is the beginning [controlling principle] of knowledge: but fools despise wisdom and instruction" (Prov. 1:7). The problem with fools isn't low IQ or deficient education. Their big problem is their heart: They won't acknowledge the Lord and submit to Him. "There is no fear of God before their eyes" (Rom. 3:18).

O–75

The only fools who are "wise fools" are Christians, because they're

63

"fools for Christ's sake" (1 Cor. 4:10). The world calls them fools, but in trusting Jesus Christ and committing their lives to Him, they've made the wisest decision anybody can make.

O–81

Forgiveness

The fire of anger, if not quenched by loving forgiveness, will spread and defile and destroy the work of God.

SS–41

An unforgiving spirit is the devil's playground, and before long it becomes the Christian's battleground.

SS–43

Learning how to forgive and forget is one of the secrets of a happy Christian life.

SS–43

When you come to God with a broken heart, confessing your sins, He will receive you the way a loving mother receives a disobedient child. He will love you and even sing to you! He will bring peace to your heart and "quiet you in His love." Yes, we suffer for our disobedience; and sometimes we carry the scars of that disobedience for the rest of our lives. But the Lord will forgive us (1 John 1:9), forget our sins, and restore us into His loving fellowship.

Dr. William Culbertson, late president of Moody Bible Institute, sometimes ended his public prayers with, "And, Lord, help us bear the consequences of forgiven sin and to end well." There are consequences to *forgiven* sin; for though God in His grace cleanses us, God in His government says, "You will reap what you have sown."

E–138

Forsaken

God has never forsaken you. You may have felt as though God abandoned you, but God has never forsaken you. If God forsook you for one second, you would die, because "in him we live, and move, and have our being" (Acts 17:28).

BB–47

Freedom

The more you become like the Lord Jesus Christ, the more it releases your potential. We have yet to see what God can do in our lives! You may think you have no gifts or abilities. You may think there are no opportunities for you. You may be discouraged. But the more you become like Jesus Christ, the more you experience

64

freedom. And the more freedom you experience, the more you release your own potential. Oh, the wonderful power and potential that God has put within you! *Freedom is life controlled by truth and motivated by love.* Bondage is life controlled by lies and motivated by selfishness. Freedom is the result of a living relationship with Jesus Christ—walking with Him, talking with Him, and learning from Him.

T–12

Satan uses lies to bring you into bondage, and that bondage leads to destruction; but God uses truth to bring you into freedom, and that freedom leads to fulfillment. In Genesis 3 Satan said to our first parents, "Yea, hath God said?" (v. 1) and then he promised them, "You will be like God" (v. 5 NIV). Satan was offering them freedom without responsibility, freedom without consequences, *and there can be no such thing.* Satan's lie is "You will be like God," and that is the lie that rules the world today. Man is his own God. The world today is worshiping "the creature more than the Creator" (Rom. 1:25). Man no longer looks at himself as a creature who must be obedient to God. Man looks at himself as the creator. Man is now his own God! God's

purpose for man is freedom, and God's method for freedom is truth.

T–8–9

Freedom is the privilege and power to become all that God wants you to become. Freedom is the opportunity to fulfill your potential to the glory of God.

T–6

You were born with a tremendous potential. When you were born again through faith in Jesus Christ, God added spiritual gifts to your natural talents. God surrounds you with opportunity. You and I are free in Jesus Christ, not to do whatever we want but to be all that God wants us to be.

T–7

Friends

We must never take our friends for granted and think that they will immediately forgive our offenses, even though forgiveness is the right thing for Christians. "A brother offended is harder to win than a strong city, and contentions are like the bars of a castle" (Prov. 18:19). It's strange but true that some of God's people will forgive offenses from unbelievers that they would never forgive if a Christian friend committed them. It takes a diamond to cut a diamond, and some

Christians have a way of putting up defenses that even the church can't break through. Matthew 18:15–35 gives us the steps to take when such things happen, and our Lord warns us that an unforgiving spirit only puts us into prison!

O–109

Fruitbearing

We need God's resources to bear fruit. But where we place our roots is paramount. Only as we grow them deeply into the spiritual resources of God's grace will we produce fruit. Make the Bible your spiritual resource. Delight in it and feed your soul with its truth. God can use you to help win the lost.

JJ–3

Fruit of the Spirit

Too many Christians try to "produce results" in their own efforts instead of abiding in Christ and allowing His life to produce the fruit.

SS–66

The difference between spiritual fruit and human "religious activity" is that the fruit brings glory to Jesus Christ. Whenever we do anything in our own strength, we have a tendency to boast about it. True spiritual fruit is so beautiful and wonderful that no man can claim credit for it: the glory must go to God.

SS–66

The Christian need not have an identity crisis. Jesus tells us who we are and why we are here. We are branches, and He is the Vine. We are here to bear fruit. Once you accept this simple fact, you are on the way to making your life meaningful and useful.

U–15

Those of us who have experienced salvation need to learn the importance of cultivating our own hearts and planting the Word. Unless we spend time planting the Word (understanding it) and cultivating it (meditating and praying), we cannot be fruitful Christians. We must be certain that our soil is free from weeds, plowed up, and ready to receive God's Word.

EEE–30

G

Gift

What we are is God's gift to us; what we do with it is our gift to Him.

F–17

Gifts, Spiritual

A spiritual gift is a God-given ability to serve God and other Christians in such a way that Christ is glorified and believers are edified.

SS–37

Giving

Giving to God and, in His name, to others, is not something that we *do*; it is the result of what we *are*. When the branch is receiving life from the Vine, *it cannot help but give*. The branch exists to give! For the branch, *giving* and *living* are synonymous. To live is to give; to give is to live. The believer cannot selfishly hold on to whatever material blessings God gives him. If he is abiding in the Vine, he cannot help but give.

U–20–21

Glory

Just as a man's wealth brings glory to his name, so God will get glory from the church because of what He has invested in us.

SS–16

God

God does not dwell in man-made temples, including church buildings (Acts 7:48–50). He dwells in the hearts of those who have trusted Christ (1 Cor. 6:19–20), and in the church collectively (Eph. 2:20–22).

SS–25

To what kind of a God do we pray when we lift our prayers to "the God of heaven"? We pray to a "great and awesome God" (Neh. 1:5 NKJV; and see 4:14; 8:6; and 9:32), who is worthy of our praise and worship. If you are experiencing great affliction (v. 3) and are about to undertake a great work (4:19; 6:3), then you need the great power (1:10), great goodness (9:25, 35), and great mercy (v. 31) of a great God. Is the God you worship big enough to handle the challenges that you face?

G–18

God originally made man in His own image. Today, man is making God in his own image.

SS–200

Godliness

To "exercise unto godliness" means to put into practice the rules and requirements for a godly life. Certainly it includes prayer and witnessing, meditation on God's Word, and the good works that the Spirit enables us to perform. It implies discipling the life, exercising the conscience (Acts 24:16), and using the "spiritual senses" God has given us (Heb. 5:14).

CCC–34

Gospel

God sometimes uses strange tools to help us pioneer the gospel. In Paul's case, there were three tools that helped him take the gospel even into the elite Praetorian Guard, Caesar's special troops: his *chains* (Phil. 1:12–14), his *critics* (Phil. 1:15–19), and his *crisis* (Phil. 1:20–26).

SS–67

The purpose of the early church was to spread the gospel and win souls, not to get involved in social action. Had the first Christians been branded as an antigovernment sect, they would have been greatly hindered in their soulwinning and their church expansion. While it is good and right for Christians to get involved in the promotion of honesty and morality in government and society, this concern must never replace the mandate to go into all the world and preach the gospel (Mark 16:15).

SS–144

Government

The individual Christian citizen might not agree with the way all of his tax money is used, and he can express himself with his voice and his vote, but he must accept the fact that God has established human government for our good (Rom. 13; 1 Tim. 2:1–6; 1 Peter 2:13–17). Even if we cannot respect the people in office, we must respect the office.

RR–152

God has established authority in this world, and when we resist authority, we are resisting God (Rom. 13:1ff). Parents are to have authority over their children (Eph. 6:1–4) and employers over their employees (Eph. 6:5–8). As citizens, we Christians should pray for those in authority (1 Tim. 2:1–4), show respect to them (1 Peter 2:11–17), and seek to glorify God in our behavior. As members of a local assembly, we should honor those who have the spiritual rule over us and seek to encourage them in their ministry (Heb. 13:7, 17; 1 Peter 5:1–6).

Human government is, in one sense, God's gift to help maintain order in the world, so that the church may minister the Word and win the lost to Christ (1 Tim. 2:1–8). We should pray daily for those in authority so that they might exercise that authority in the will of God. It is a serious thing for a Christian to oppose the law, and he must be sure he is in the will of God when he does it. He should also do it in a manner that glori-

fies Christ, so that innocent people (including unsaved government employees) might not be made to suffer.

SS–452

Grace

Grace is not simply a supplement to our strength, for we have no strength of our own. Grace turns our weakness into power for the glory of God. "For when I am weak, then am I strong" (2 Cor. 12:10).

Y–51

Grace and *faith* go together, because the only way to experience grace and salvation is through faith (Eph. 2:8–9).

SS–9

It is not God's love that saves the sinner; it is God's grace. God in His grace gives us what we do not deserve, and God in His mercy does not give us what we do deserve.

SS–160

We cannot make ourselves acceptable to God; but He, by His grace, makes us accepted in Christ.

SS–11

Sin made us poor, but grace makes us rich.

SS–12

Positionally, we are complete in Christ, but practically, we enjoy only the grace that we apprehend by faith.

SS–33

We are alive in Christ, not dead in sins; therefore "put off the old man . . . and put on the new man" (Eph. 4:22, 24). Take off the grave-clothes and put on the grace-clothes!

SS–39

Two words in the Christian vocabulary are often confused: *grace* and *mercy*. God in His grace gives me what I do not deserve. Yet God in His mercy does not give me what I do deserve. Grace is God's favor shown to undeserving sinners. The reason the gospel is *good* news is because of grace: God is willing and able to save all who will trust Jesus Christ.

SS–106

Jesus Christ has *fullness of grace and truth* (John 1:16–17). Grace is God's favor and kindness bestowed on those who do not deserve it and cannot earn it. If God dealt with us only according to truth, none of us would survive; but He deals with us on the basis of grace *and* truth. Jesus Christ, in His life, death, and resurrection, met all the demands of the Law; now God is free to share fullness of grace with those who trust Christ. Grace without truth would be deceitful, and truth without grace would be condemning.

RR–286

Keep in mind that God's grace involves something more than man's salvation. We not only are saved by grace, but we are to live by grace (1 Cor. 15:10). We stand in grace; it is the foundation for the Christian life (Rom. 5:1–2). Grace gives us the strength we need to be victorious soldiers (2 Tim. 2:1–4). Grace enables us to suffer without complaining, and even to use that suffering for God's glory (2 Cor. 12:1–10). When a Christian turns away from living by God's grace, he must depend on his own power. This leads to failure and disappointment. This is what Paul means by "fallen from grace" (Gal. 5:4)—moving out of the sphere of grace into the sphere of Law, ceasing to depend on God's resources and depending on our own resources.

RR–684

God's grace does not fail, but we can fail to depend on God's grace.

SS–325

Grandchildren

God has no grandchildren. Each of us must be born into the family of God through personal faith in Jesus Christ (John 1:11–13).

RR–431

Growth

The mind grows by taking in, but the heart grows giving out.

S–15

Guilt

Satan wants you to feel guilty. Your heavenly Father wants you to know that you are forgiven. Satan knows that if you live under a dark cloud of guilt, you will not be able to witness effectively or serve the Lord with power and blessing. Sad to say, there are some churches that major in guilt. They seem to feel that unless a Christian goes home from a service feeling like a failure, the services have not been a blessing. "Every time we go to church," a lady wrote me, "the pastor spanks us. What should we do?" To be sure, there is a place for proper spiritual conviction; but we must not major on guilt. To do so is to play right into the devil's hands.

AAA–87

H

Happen

Someone has said that there are three kinds of men in the world: those who make things happen, those who watch things happen, and those who have no idea anything is happening. This is true in the spiritual realm. There are a few men who are being used of God to make things happen; there are many more who watch the others work; and there are multitudes who seem to be blind and deaf, unaware that God is even at work in this world!

CCC–55

Happiness

John 13:17 is the key—"If ye know these things, happy are ye if ye do them." The sequence is important: humbleness, holiness, then happiness. Aristotle defined happiness as "good fortune joined to virtue . . . a life that is both agree-able and secure." That might do for a philosopher, but it will never do for a Christian believer! Happiness is the by-product of a life that is lived in the will of God. When we humbly serve others, walk in God's paths of holiness, and do what He tells us, then we will enjoy happiness.

RR–346

Harvest

Ours is a ministry of faith, and we don't always see the results. The harvest is not the end of the meeting or of the church year. The harvest is the end of the age, and the Lord of the harvest will see to it that His good and faithful servants will get their just rewards.

Z–23

Healing

The greatest need a person has is not physical healing, but spiri-

72

tual healing. Sin ravages the soul far worse than disease ravages the body.

Y–112

Heart

Change the heart and you change the speech.

SS–42

Fill the heart with the love of Christ so that only truth and purity can come out of the mouth.

SS–42

The heart of every problem is the problem of the heart, and only God's Spirit and God's Word can change and control the heart.

SS–145

Heaven

Christians are the citizens of heaven, and while we are on earth we ought to behave like heaven's citizens.

SS–72

Some people have the idea that, no matter how they lived as a Christian, when they die and go to heaven, they will be just like the spiritual giants of the faith. But that idea is not true. An old Puritan preacher used to say, "Every vessel in heaven will be filled, but some vessels will be larger than others." Why will some vessels be larger than others? Because those people walked with the Lord and enjoyed the firstfruits of the Spirit here on earth. You and I need to prepare right now for the blessings of heaven.

H–49

Heaven was at the cross because the cross is the only way to heaven. The way to God was opened, not by the life of Jesus or the example of Jesus, not even by the teaching of Jesus, but by the death of Jesus on the cross. "For Christ also suffered once for sins, the just for the unjust, that He might bring us to God . . . ." (1 Peter 3:18 NKJV). We have "boldness to enter the Holiest by the blood of Jesus" (Heb. 10:19 NKJV).

UU–43

The believer's sanctuary is in heaven. His Father is in heaven and his Savior is in heaven. His citizenship is in heaven (Phil. 3:20) and his treasures should be in heaven (Matt. 6:19ff). And his hope is in heaven. The true believer walks by faith, not by sight. No matter what may happen on earth, a believer can be confident because everything is settled in heaven.

SS–312

Since our citizenship is in heaven and our home is in heaven, we as

God's pilgrims must cultivate a "heavenly mind" as we journey here on earth. We must constantly be looking for the Savior (Phil. 3:20). This does not mean that we neglect our earthly responsibilities and, as D. L. Moody used to say, become "so heavenly minded that we are no earthly good." Quite the contrary is true. People who are looking for their Lord ought to be *more faithful* as parents, children, employees, citizens, friends, and servants of God.

It was this "heavenly hope" that motivated men of faith like Abraham, Isaac, and Jacob; for they "looked for a city . . . whose builder and maker is God" (Heb. 11:10; note vv. 13–16). The eyes of God's pilgrims must not look *back* to the old life (Luke 9:62), or look *around* at the distractions of the world (Gen. 13:10–11). They must focus *above*, by faith, and be fixed on the Lord Jesus Christ (Heb. 12:1–2). Because we have been raised with Christ, we should "seek those things which are above" (Col. 3:1ff.).

Q–48

For the Christian, heaven isn't simply a *destination:* it's a *motivation.*

K–9

Hell

If you've done any witnessing, you've probably met people who seem to have no concept of the tragedy of sin and the awfulness of hell. "I don't mind going to hell," they say rather flippantly. "I'll have lots of company." But there is no company in hell, because hell is a place of eternal isolation and loneliness. Like the lepers outside the camp, lost sinners will dwell alone; they will be alone forever.

J–59

One of the agonies of hell will be the remembrance of opportunities wasted.

RR–227

High Priest

What happens when we who have been saved are tempted to sin? Jesus Christ stands ready to help us! He was tempted when He was on earth, but no temptation ever conquered Him. Because He has defeated every enemy, He is able to give us the grace that we need to overcome temptation. The word "succour" (Heb. 2:18) literally means "to run to the cry of a child." It means "to bring help when it is needed." Angels are able to *serve* us (Heb. 1:14), but they are not able to *succour* us in our times of temptation. Only Jesus Christ can do that, and He can do it because He became a man and suffered and died.

It might be good at this point to explain the difference between our

Lord's ministry as High Priest and His ministry as Advocate (1 John 2:1). As our High Priest, our Lord is able to give us grace to keep us from sinning when we are tempted. If we do sin, then He as our Advocate represents us before the throne of God and forgives us when we sincerely confess our sins to Him (1 John 1:5–2:2). Both of these ministries are involved in His present work of intercession; and it is this intercessory ministry that is the guarantee of our eternal salvation (note that in Heb. 7:25 it is "*to* the uttermost"—i.e., eternally—and not "*from* the uttermost").

SS–284–85

This open way into God's presence is "new" (recent, fresh) and not a part of the Old Covenant that "waxeth [grows] old [and] is ready to vanish away" (Heb. 8:13). It is "living" because Christ "ever liveth to make intercession" for us (Heb. 7:25). Christ is the new and living way! We come to God through Him, our High Priest over the house of God (the church, see Heb. 3:6). When His flesh was torn on the cross, and His life sacrificed, God tore the veil in the temple. This symbolized the new and living way now opened for all who believe.

On the basis of these assurances—that we have boldness to enter because we have a living High Priest—we have an "open invitation" to enter the presence of God. The Old Covenant high priest *visited* the holy of holies once a year, but we are invited to *dwell in the presence of God* every moment of each day. What a tremendous privilege! Consider what is involved in this invitation.

SS–315

Holiness

Happiness, not holiness, is the chief pursuit of most people today, including many professed Christians. They want Jesus to solve their problems and carry their burdens, but they don't want Him to control their lives and change their character. It doesn't disturb them that eight times in the Bible, God said to His people, "Be holy, for I am holy," *and He means it.*

J–9

God's holiness isn't simply the absence of defilement, a negative thing. The holiness of God is positive and active. It's God's perfect nature at work in accomplishing God's perfect will.

J–11

One of the essential differences between mere outward piety and true holiness is that piety makes you conform to a system, while true holiness conforms you to Christ *and develops your own individuality.*

DD–104

Holy Spirit

Every true believer possesses the Holy Spirit (Rom. 8:9; 1 Cor. 6:19–20), and it is through the Spirit's power that the Christian is able to function in the world.

SS–9

Not to know and depend on the Holy Spirit's provision is to live a life of spiritual poverty.

SS–9

Unless you have the *witness* of the Spirit (Rom. 8:15–16), you cannot draw on the *wealth* of the Spirit.

SS–10

Just as a signature on a letter attests to the genuineness of the document, so the presence of the Spirit proves the believer is genuine. "If any man have not the Spirit of Christ, he is none of his" (Rom. 8:9).

SS–13

The Holy Spirit is God's first installment to guarantee to His children that He will finish His work and eventually bring them to glory.

SS–13

The Holy Spirit reveals truth to us from the Word, and then gives us the wisdom to understand and apply it. He also gives us the power—the enablement—to practice the truth (Eph. 3:14–21).

SS–14

The inability to see and understand spiritual things is not the fault of the intelligence but of the heart. The eyes of the heart must be opened by the Spirit of God.

SS–15

The righteousness of the Law, revealing God's holiness, is still God's standard. But this is fulfilled in the believer by the Holy Spirit.

SS–24

It is only when we yield to the Spirit and let Him control the inner man that we succeed in living to the glory of God.

SS–32

Christians today do not get their spiritual knowledge *immediately* from the Holy Spirit, but *mediately* through the Spirit teaching the Word.

SS–37

The baptism of the Spirit means that I belong to Christ's body. The filling of the Spirit means that my body belongs to Christ.

SS–48

76

If our homes are to be a heaven on earth, then we must be controlled by the Holy Spirit.

SS–48

The important thing is that we are filled with the Spirit of God. The Spirit of God has come—that is a settled matter. The Spirit of God has baptized believers into the church—that, too, is a settled matter. The Spirit of God can fill us, moment by moment, and enable us to glorify God. The Spirit of God can speak through us in languages people understand.

Has your tongue been set on fire from heaven? It is not important that you have some miraculous, ecstatic experience. It is important that the Holy Spirit use you to bear witness to Jesus Christ and to share the gospel with the whole world.

H–66

Certainly the church today needs a new filling of the Spirit of God. Apart from the ministry of the Spirit, believers can't witness with power (Acts 1:8), understand the Scriptures (John 16:13), glorify Christ (v. 14), pray in the will of God (Rom. 8:26–27), or develop Christian character (Gal. 5:22–23). We need to be praying for revival, a deeper working of the Spirit in His people, leading to confession of sin, repentance, forgiveness, and unity.

A–60

Jesus had a great deal to say about the Holy Spirit in His Upper Room message, for apart from the help of the Spirit of God, we cannot live the Christian life as God would have us live it. We must know who the Holy Spirit is, what He does, and how He does it.

The Holy Spirit is given two special names by our Lord: "another Comforter" and "the Spirit of truth." The Greek word translated "Comforter" is *parakletos* and it is used only by John (14:16, 26; 15:26; 16:7; 1 John 2:1). It means "called alongside to assist." The Holy Spirit does not work instead of us, or in spite of us, but in us and through us.

Our English word *comfort* comes from two Latin words meaning "with strength." We usually think of "comfort" as soothing someone, consoling him or her; and to some extent this is true. But true comfort strengthens us to face life bravely and keep on going. It does not rob us of responsibility or make it easy for us to give up. Some translations call the Holy Spirit "the Encourager," and this is a good choice of words. *Parakletos* is translated "Advocate" in 1 John 2:1. An "advocate" is one who represents you at court and stands at your side to plead your case.

RR–352

Home, Christian

Our Christian homes are to be pictures of Christ's relationship to His church. Each believer is a member of Christ's body, and each believer is to help nourish the body in love (Eph. 4:16). We are one with Christ. The church is His body and His bride, and the Christian home is a divinely ordained illustration of this relationship. This certainly makes marriage a serious matter.

SS–51

When Christian couples try to imitate the world and get their standards from Hollywood instead of from heaven, there will be trouble in the home. But if both partners will imitate Jesus Christ in His submission and obedience, and His desire to serve others, then there will be triumph and joy in the home. A psychiatrist friend of mine states that the best thing a Christian husband can do is pattern himself after Jesus Christ. In Christ we see a beautiful blending of strength and tenderness, and that is what it takes to be a successful husband.

SS–408

An unsaved husband will not be converted by preaching or nagging in the home. The phrase "without the word" does not mean "without the Word of God," because salvation comes through the Word (John 5:24). It means "without talk, without a lot of speaking." Christian wives who preach at their husbands only drive them farther from the Lord. I know one zealous wife who used to keep religious radio programs on all evening, usually very loud, so that her unsaved husband would "hear the truth." She only made it easier for him to leave home and spend his evenings with his friends.

SS–407

Humility

Humility is that grace that, when you know you have it, you have lost it. The truly humble person knows himself and accepts himself (Rom. 12:3).

SS–73

Humility is not thinking poorly of oneself. Rather, it is having the proper estimate of oneself in the will of God (Rom. 12:3). The person with humbleness of mind thinks of others first and not of himself.

SS–138

Every Christian needs a "valley gate," for God opposes the proud but gives grace to the humble

(1 Peter 5:5–6). It is only as we yield to Christ and serve others that we can truly enter into the fullness of the life He has for us (Phil. 2:1–11).

G–44

Humor

If the preacher has a sense of humor, he had better dedicate it to the Lord and let the Spirit direct him in its use. For true humor can become a toy to play with, a tool to build with, or a dangerous weapon to fight with.

VV–100

Hunger

If a man wants to master a skill, he must have a deep desire to do so, or he will fail. Perhaps his motives are mixed, but if there is a hunger for achievement, he will have an easier time. Change the hunger, and you change the man; control the hunger, and you control the man. Jesus Christ wants to create in us a deep hunger for God, a hunger for holiness. It is this hunger that will change and control our lives as we satisfy it in Jesus Christ.

DD–104

Husband/Wife

God does all things "decently and in order" (1 Cor. 14:40). If He did not have a chain of command in society, we would have chaos. The fact that the woman is to submit to her husband does not suggest that the man is better than the woman. It only means that the man has the responsibility of headship and leadership in the home.

Headship is not dictatorship or lordship. It is loving leadership. In fact, both the husband and the wife must be submitted to the *Lord* and to *each other* (Eph. 5:21). It is a mutual respect under the lordship of Jesus Christ.

SS–142

The husband must make time to be home with his wife. Christian workers and church officers who get too busy running around solving other people's problems may end up creating problems of their own at home. One survey revealed that the average husband and wife had thirty-seven minutes a week together in actual communication! Is it any wonder that marriages fall apart after the children grow up and leave home? The husband and wife are left alone—to live with strangers!

"Dwell with them" also suggests that the husband provide for the physical and material needs of the home. While it is not wrong for a wife to have a job or career, her first responsibility is to care for the home

(Titus 2:4–5). It is the husband who should provide (1 Tim. 5:8).

SS–410

Chivalry may be dead, but every husband must be a "knight in shining armor" who treats his wife like a princess. (By the way, the name Sarah means "princess.") Peter did not suggest that a wife is "the weaker vessel" mentally, morally, or spiritually, but rather physically. There are exceptions, of course, but generally speaking, the man is the stronger of the two when it comes to physical accomplishments. The husband should treat his wife like an expensive, beautiful, fragile vase, in which is a precious treasure.

SS–410

Twice in this paragraph Peter reminded Christian wives that they were to be submissive to their husbands (1 Peter 3:1, 5). The word translated "subjection" is a military term that means "to place under rank." God has a place for everything; He has ordained various levels of authority (see 1 Peter 2:13–14). He has ordained that the husband be the head of the home (Eph. 5:21ff.) and that, as he submits to Christ, his wife should submit to him. Headship is not dictatorship, but the loving exercise of divine authority under the lordship of Jesus Christ.

Peter gave three reasons why a Christian wife should submit to her husband, even if the husband (as in this case) is not saved.

God has commanded it because, in His wisdom, He knows that this is the best arrangement for a happy, fulfilling marriage. Subjection does not mean that the wife is inferior to the husband. In fact, in 1 Peter 3:7, Peter made it clear that the husband and wife are "heirs together." The man and woman are made by the same Creator out of the same basic material, and both are made in God's image. God gave dominion to both Adam and Eve (Gen. 1:28), and in Jesus Christ Christian mates are one (Gal. 3:28).

Submission has to do with order and authority, not evaluation. For example, the slaves in the average Roman household were superior in many ways to their masters, but they still had to be under authority. The buck private in the army may be a better person than the five-star general, but he is still a buck private. Even Christ Himself became a servant and submitted to God's will. There is nothing degrading about submitting to authority or accepting God's order. If anything, it is the first step toward fulfillment. And Ephesians 5:21 makes it clear that *both* husband

and wife must first be submitted to Jesus Christ.

Husbands and wives must be partners, not competitors. After a wedding ceremony, I often privately say to the bride and groom, "Now, remember, from now on it's no longer *mine* or *yours*, but *ours*." This explains why Christians must always marry other Christians, for a believer cannot enter into any kind of deep "oneness" with an unbeliever (2 Cor. 6:14–18).

SS–408

The husband must be the "thermostat" in the home, setting the emotional and spiritual temperature. The wife often is the "thermometer," letting him know what that temperature is! Both are necessary. The husband who is sensitive to his wife's feelings will not only make her happy, but will also grow himself and help his children live in a home that honors God.

SS–411

Hypocrisy

Hypocrisy means deliberately pretending. None of us lives up to his ideals; none of us is all that he would like to be or all that he could be in Christ. But that is not hypocrisy. Falling short of our ideals is not hypocrisy. Pretending we have reached our ideals when we have not—that is hypocrisy.

H–35

George MacDonald wrote, "Half of the misery in the world comes from trying to *look*, instead of trying to *be*, what one is not." The name that Jesus gave to this practice is "hypocrisy," which simply means "wearing a mask, playing the actor." We must not think that failure to reach our ideals is hypocrisy, because no believer lives up to all that he or she knows or has in the Lord. Hypocrisy is *deliberate* deception, trying to make people think we are more spiritual than we really are.

RR–421

81

I

Idol, Idolatry

The essence of idolatry is worshiping and serving something other than God; living, if you please, on substitutes.

Y–23–24

When I was a child in Sunday school, the superintendent often chose the song "Whiter Than Snow" for us to sing in general assembly. While we sang "Break down every idol/Cast out every foe," I confess that I didn't understand at the time what I was singing; but now I understand. *The Lord will not share my life if there are rival gods in my heart. He will not permit me to compromise with the enemy.* When you grasp this truth, you also better understand His admonition in 2 Corinthians 6:14–7:1.

P–81

The tragedy of idolatry is that a dead image can do a worshiper no good because it is not genuine. Hebrew writers in the Old Testament called idols "nothing, vain things, vapors, emptiness." An idol is a lifeless, useless *substitute* for the real thing.

The Psalms contain caustic indictments of idolatry (Pss. 115:1–8; 135:15–18). To human vision, an idol looks real—eyes, ears, mouth, nose, hands, feet—but these are but useless imitations of the real thing. The eyes are blind, the ears are deaf, the mouth is silent, the hands and feet are paralyzed. But the real tragedy is that "those who make them will become like them; everyone who trusts in them" (Ps. 115:8 NASB). We become like the god we worship!

82

This is the secret of the life that is real. Because we have met the true God, through His Son Jesus Christ, we are in contact with reality. Our fellowship is with a God who is genuine.

SS–531

The thing we serve is the thing we worship! Whatever controls our lives and "calls the signals" is our god.

This explains why God warns us against the sin of idolatry. Not only is it a violation of His commandment (Exod. 20:1–6), but it is a subtle way for Satan to take control of us.

SS–532

Anything that we trust other than the Lord becomes our god and therefore is an idol. It may be our training, experience, job, money, friends, or position. One of the best ways to find out whether we have idols in our lives is to ask ourselves, "Where do I instinctively turn when I face a decision or need to solve a problem?" Do we reach for the phone to call a friend? Do we assure ourselves that we can handle the situation ourselves? Or do we turn to God and seek His will and His help?

When the storm starts blowing, the idols will blow away like chaff. They are "vanity," which means "nothingness." The storm does not make a person; it shows what the person is made of and where his or her faith lies. If we make the Lord our refuge, we have nothing to fear.

C–151

Ignorance

A confession of ignorance is the first step toward true knowledge. "And if anyone thinks that he knows anything, he knows nothing yet as he ought to know" (1 Cor. 8:2 NKJV). The person who wants to learn God's truth must possess honesty and humility. Harvard philosopher Alfred North Whitehead said, "Not ignorance, but ignorance of ignorance, is the death of knowledge."

N–102

Imagination

Imagination is a womb that is impregnated with the old so that it might give birth to the new. It is the bridge that links the world around you with the world within you. It's also one of the bridges between your right brain and your left brain, so that *vision* has *super-vision* and doesn't become just *visionary.*

KK–25

Inheritance

A "living hope" is one that has life in it and therefore can give life to us. Because it has life, it grows and becomes greater and more beautiful as time goes on. Time destroys most hopes; they fade and then die. But the passing of time only makes a Christian's hope that much more glorious.

Peter called this hope *an inheritance* (1 Peter 1:4). As the children of the King, we share His inheritance in glory (Rom. 8:17–18; Eph. 1:9–12). We are included in Christ's last will and testament, and we share the glory with Him (John 17:22–24).

Note the description of this inheritance, for it is totally unlike any earthly inheritance. For one thing, it is *incorruptible*, which means that nothing can ruin it. Because it is *undefiled*, it cannot be stained or cheapened in any way. It will never grow old because it is eternal; it cannot wear out, nor can it disappoint us in any way.

In 1 Peter 1:5 and 9, this inheritance is called "salvation." The believer is already saved through faith in Christ (Eph. 2:8–9), but the completion of that salvation awaits the return of the Savior. Then we shall have new bodies and enter into a new environment, the heavenly city. In 1 Peter 1:7, Peter called this hope "the appearing of Jesus Christ." Paul called this the "blessed hope" (Titus 2:13).

What a thrilling thing it is to know that we were born for glory! When we were born again, we exchanged the passing glory of man for the eternal glory of God!

SS–392

We are "joint-heirs with Christ" (Rom. 8:17), which means that He cannot claim His inheritance apart from us!

SS–12

Integrity

Integrity is to personal or corporate character what health is to the body or 20/20 vision is to the eyes. A person with integrity is not divided (that's *duplicity*) or merely pretending (that's *hypocrisy*). He or she is "whole"; life is "put together," and things are working together harmoniously. People with integrity have nothing to hide and nothing to fear. Their lives are open books. They are integers.

WW–21

Jesus made it clear that integrity involves the whole of the inner person: the heart, the mind, and the will (Matt. 6:19–24). The person with integrity has a *single heart*. He doesn't try to love God and the world at the same time. His heart is in heaven, and that's where his treasure is. "Do not love the world, nor the things in the world. If anyone loves the world, the love of the Father is not in him" (1 John 2:15 NASB). An integrated person takes this command seriously: "You shall love the Lord your God with all your heart" (Matt. 22:37 NASB).

WW–21–22

When *hypocrisy* (lying to others) and *duplicity* (lying to oneself) start to take over, integrity gradually erodes until it is finally destroyed. The result is always *apostasy* (making God a liar), and gradually the light becomes darkness. And all this takes place *while the person or the ministry is maintaining what appears to be a faithful relationship with God.*

WW–25

Many ministries today are governed by popularity and not by integrity, by statistics and not by Scripture.

WW–69

85

J

Jealousy

Jealousy is a sin if it means being envious of what others have and wanting to possess it, but it's a virtue if it means cherishing what we have and wanting to protect it. A faithful husband and wife are jealous *over* one another and do everything they can to keep their relationship exclusive. "Jealous" and "zealous" come from the same root, for when you're jealous over someone, you're zealous to protect the relationship.

A–98

Jesus Christ

No matter where you turn in the Old Testament record, you meet Jesus Christ.

Y–47

Christ! Because "He is before all things," He can hold all things together. Again, this is another affirmation that Jesus Christ is God. Only God exists before all of Creation, and only God can make Creation cohere. To make Jesus Christ less than God is to dethrone Him.

SS–116

There is no need to add anything to the person or work of Jesus Christ. To add anything is to take away from His glory. To give Him prominence instead of preeminence is to dethrone Him.

SS–119

The Christian is not subject in any way to the Old Testament legal system, *nor can it do him any good spiritually.* Jesus Christ *alone* is sufficient for our every spiritual need, for all of God's fullness is in Him. We are identified with Jesus Christ because He is the Head of the body (Col. 1:18) and we are the

86

members of the body (1 Cor. 12:12–13).

SS–126

Christ not only died *for* us (substitution), but we died *with* Him (identification). Christ not only died *for* sin, bearing its penalty; but He died *unto* sin, breaking its power. Because we are "in Christ" through the work of the Holy Spirit (1 Cor. 12:13), we died with Christ. This means that we can have victory over the old sin nature that wants to control us. "How shall we, that are dead to sin, live any longer therein?" (Rom. 6:2).

SS–133

If Jesus Christ is the preeminent One in our lives, then we will love each other, submit to each other, obey, and treat one another fairly in the Lord.

SS–145

We should beware of any teaching that claims to give us "something more" than we already have in Christ. All of God's fullness is in Him, and He has perfectly equipped us for the life that God wants us to live. We do not live and grow by *addition,* but by *appropriation.*

SS–154

The Lord Jesus Christ died for sinners. He died actually, He died confidently, He died willingly, and He died victoriously. He did not die for His own sin because He had none. He died for the sins of the world. Someday you are going to die. Usually people die just the way they lived. To be sure, God can work and people can be saved at the last minute. I have led people on their deathbeds to Christ. *But don't take that chance.* Don't gamble with eternity.

BB–72

You can belong to all sorts of weird religious groups today and not suffer much opposition from family and friends, but the minute you bring the name of Jesus into the picture, and share the gospel, somebody will start to oppose you. His name is still hated.

RR 156

To "know Christ" means to have a personal relationship with Him through faith. It is this experience that Jesus mentions in John 17:3. You and I know *about* many people, even people who lived centuries ago, but we know personally very few. "Christianity *is* Christ." Salvation is knowing Him in a personal way.

SS–84

"Express image" (Heb. 1:3) carries the idea of "the exact imprint."

Our English word *character* comes from the Greek word translated "image." Literally, Jesus Christ is "the exact representation of the very substance of God" (see Col. 2:9). Only Jesus could honestly say, "He that hath seen Me hath seen the Father" (John 14:9). When you see Christ, you see the glory of God (John 1:14).

SS–280

Creator, Prophet, Priest, and King—Jesus Christ is superior to all of the prophets and servants of God who have ever appeared on the sacred pages of the Scriptures.

SS–280

The term "firstborn" in the Bible does not always mean "born first." God made Solomon the firstborn (Ps. 89:27) even though Solomon is listed *tenth* in the official genealogy (1 Chron. 3:1–5). The title is one of rank and honor, for the firstborn receives the inheritance and the special blessing. Christ is the "Firstborn of all creation" (Col. 1:15 NASB) because He created all things; and He is the highest of all who came back from the dead (Col. 1:18). When He came into the world, the angels worshiped Him (quoted from Deut. 32:43 in the Septuagint: "Heavens, rejoice with Him, let the sons of God pay Him homage!"). God commanded them to do so, which proves that Jesus Christ is God; for none of God's angels would worship a mere creature.

SS–281

Major on Jesus Christ. Make Him the preeminent One in your life. For you have all things *in* Him, *with* Him, and *through* Him—and nothing is greater than that.

CCC–62

I find that many people are miserable because they don't obey the admonition of Hebrews 12:2: "fixing our eyes on Jesus." They spend so much time looking at themselves, their circumstances, and other people that they fail to do what Ruth did, namely, center their attention on their Master. Instead of resting in His perfections, they focus on their own imperfections. Instead of seeing His spiritual riches, they complain about their bankruptcy. They go to church "to get their needs met," instead of going to church to worship the God who is greater than any need. They need to heed the counsel of the little poem a radio listener sent me years ago:

Look at self and be distressed,
Look at others and be
   depressed,
Look at Jesus and you'll be
   blessed!

D–33

Jesus, the Shepherd

The Good Shepherd *died* for the sheep and the Great Shepherd *lives* for the sheep.

PP–34

Jews

My friend, the late Dr. Jacob Gartenhaus, gifted missionary to his own people, used to say, "We Jews are waterproof and fireproof; God has blessed us so that nobody can successfully curse us, and we shall be here long after our enemies have perished." God knows what the nations have done to the Jews, and He will one day settle accounts. Meanwhile, believers must pray for the peace of Jerusalem (Ps. 122:6) and lovingly witness to them in word and deed that Jesus is indeed their Messiah and Lord.

A–63

Joy

Paul did not find his joy in ideal circumstances; he found his joy in winning others to Christ.

SS–67

No matter how you look at it, nothing can steal a man's joy if he possesses the single mind! "For to me to live is Christ, and to die is gain" (Phil. 1:21).

SS–70

The secret of joy in spite of circumstances is *the single mind.* The secret of joy in spite of people is *the submissive mind.* The key verse is: "Let nothing be done through strife or vainglory; but in lowliness of mind let each esteem others better [more important] than themselves" (Phil. 2:3). In Philippians 1, it is "Christ first" and in Philippians 2 it is "others next." Paul the soul-winner in Philippians 1 becomes Paul the servant in Philippians 2.

SS–73

Many people today are the slaves of "things," and as a result do not experience real Christian joy.

SS–84

We often use the words *joy* and *happiness* interchangeably, but a distinction should be made. Happiness often depends on happenings. If circumstances are encouraging and people are kind, we are happy. But joy is independent of both circumstances and people. The most joyful epistle Paul wrote was Philippians, and he wrote it from jail as he faced the possibility of being martyred for his faith.

SS–113

When circumstances are difficult, we should exhibit *joyful* patience; and when people are hard to live with, we should reveal *joyful* long-suffering. There is a kind of patience that "endures but does not enjoy."

SS–113

Joy in life is not the absence of sorrow. The Arabs have a motto, "All sunshine makes a desert." If God were to insulate us from sorrow, we would never grow or develop mature character. Heaven is a place of all joy and no sorrow, and hell is a place of all sorrow and no joy. But this present life is a mingling of the two. The fact that Jesus could have joy in the midst of sorrow is proof that we can experience this too.

XX–94

The world's joy is temporary and artificial; and when the joy is gone, people are left with even greater weakness and emptiness. But the joy that comes from the Lord is real and lasting and enriches our lives. God doesn't give us joy *instead* of sorrow, or joy *in spite* of sorrow, but joy *in the midst* of sorrow. It is not *substitution* but *transformation*.

G–103

Judgment

What does Enoch's prophecy (Jude 14–15) say about the coming judgment? It will be a *personal* judgment: God Himself will come to judge the world. He will not send a famine or a flood, nor will He assign the task to an angel. He Himself will come. This shows the seriousness of the event, and also its finality. "Behold, the judge standeth before the door" (James 5:9).

Though it is a personal judgment, our Lord will not judge alone; the saints of God will be with Him. The word *saints* in Jude 14 means "holy ones" and can also refer to the angels (Deut. 33:2; Matt. 25:31). However, we know from Revelation 19:14; Colossians 3:4; and 1 Thessalonians 3:13 that the people of God will accompany the Lord when He returns to earth to defeat His enemies and establish His righteous kingdom (cf. 1 Cor. 6:2–3). Over the centuries, the people of God have suffered at the hands of the ungodly, but one day the tables will be turned.

It will be a *universal* judgment. He will execute judgment "upon all"—none will escape. Just as the Flood destroyed all who were outside the ark, and the fire and brimstone destroyed all in Sodom and Gomorrah except Lot and his wife and two daughters, so the last judgment will encompass all the ungodly. The word *ungodly* is used four times in this one verse! It will be "the day of judgment and perdi-

90

tion [ruin, destruction] of ungodly men" (2 Peter 3:7).

It will be a *just* judgment. God will convict ("convince") them of their sins, declare them guilty, pass sentence on them, and then execute the punishment. There will be a Judge, Jesus Christ (John 5:22), but no jury. There will be prosecution, but no defense; for every mouth will be stopped (Rom. 3:19). There will be a sentence, but no appeal, for there can be no higher court than God's final judgment. The entire procedure will be just, for the righteous Son of God will be in charge.

SS–557

Justification

Justification is the act of God whereby He declares the believing sinner righteous in Christ on the basis of the finished work of Christ on the cross. Each part of this definition is important, so we must consider it carefully.

To begin with, justification is an act, not a process. There are no degrees of justification; each believer has the same right standing before God. Also, justification is something *God* does, not man. No sinner can justify himself before God. Most important, justification does not mean that God *makes* us righteous, but that He *declares* us

righteous. Justification is a legal matter. God puts the righteousness of Christ on our record in the place of our own sinfulness. And nobody can change this record.

Do not confuse justification and sanctification. Sanctification is the process whereby God makes the believer more and more like Christ. Sanctification may change from day to day. Justification never changes. When the sinner trusts Christ, God declares him righteous, and that declaration will never be repealed. God looks on us and deals with us as though we had never sinned at all!

RR–522

Adam's sin brought judgment and condemnation; but Christ's work on the cross brings justification. When Adam sinned, he was declared unrighteous and condemned. When a sinner trusts Christ, he is justified—declared righteous in Christ.

Our justification is the result of a living union with Christ. And this union ought to result in a new kind of life, a righteous life of obedience to God. Our union with Adam made us sinners; our union with Christ enables us to "reign in life."

RR–529

In justification, God *declares* the believing sinner righteous; He does

91

not *make* him righteous. (Of course, real justification leads to a changed life, which is what James 2 is all about.) Before the sinner trusts Christ, he stands GUILTY before God; but the moment he trusts Christ, he is declared NOT GUILTY and he can never be called GUILTY again!

Justification is not simply "forgiveness," because a person could be forgiven and then go out and sin and become guilty. Once you have been "justified by faith" you can never be held guilty before God.

Justification is also different from "pardon," because a pardoned criminal still has a record. When the sinner is justified by faith, *his past sins are remembered against him no more,* and God no longer puts his sins on record (see Ps. 32:1–2; Rom. 4:1–8).

RR–695

Justification is by grace not by human merit. It is by faith and not by works—even religious works. It is by the blood of Jesus Christ, for He had to die so that our sins might be forgiven. And justification is unto life. It is not separated from life, it changes our lives.

CC–21

The marks of justification in the believer's life are revealed in *relationships.* If you are truly justified by faith, then you are going to have a right relationship with *God,* a right relationship to *circumstances,* and a right relationship to *other people.*

CC–22

K

Kingdom of God

What does it mean to seek first the kingdom of God and His righteousness? It means that God is first in our lives. First thing in the morning, we talk to God in prayer and worship. We turn to Him in the Word. The first day of every week we are in church. The first thing in our lives—the most important thing—is to please Him. When God is first and we are worshiping Him and not things, then people and things fall into their proper place.

T–81–82

Knowledge

The Corinthians were especially rich in spiritual gifts (2 Cor. 8:7), but were not using these gifts in a spiritual manner. The fact that God has called us, set us apart, and enriched us ought to encourage us to live holy lives.

RR–569

Why are the weak Christians upset with strong believers when their position is so logical? Because you don't always solve every problem with logic. The little child who is afraid of the dark will not be assured by arguments, especially if the adult (or older brother) adopts a superior attitude. Knowledge can be a weapon to fight with or a tool to build with, depending on how it is used. If it "puffs up" then it cannot "build up [edify]."

A know-it-all attitude is only an evidence of ignorance. The person who really knows truth is only too conscious of how much he does not know. Furthermore, it is one thing to know *doctrine* and quite something else to know *God*. It is possible to grow in Bible knowledge and yet not grow in grace or in one's personal relationship with God. The test is *love*.

RR–595

It is possible to grow in knowledge and not grow in grace. I have met people who have a great deal of Bible knowledge, but nobody can get along with them. They run from church to church, creating problems and trying to be important. It is possible to grow in knowledge but not grow in grace. However, when we are growing in knowledge, taught by the Holy Spirit, then we have to grow in grace. The same Holy Spirit who wrote the Word of God *writes* the Word of God in our hearts and enables us to reveal the fruit of the Spirit.

CC–9

L

Law

Jesus not only took our sins to the cross (1 Peter 2:24), but He also took the Law to the cross and nailed it there, forever out of the way. The Law was certainly against us, because it was impossible for us to meet its holy demands. Even though God never gave the Ten Commandments to the Gentiles, the righteous demands of the Law—God's holy standards—were "written in their hearts" (Rom. 2:12–16).

SS–128

The Law reveals sin and warns of the consequences of sin—but it has no power to prevent sin or redeem the sinner. Only grace can do that.

SS–129

The Law cannot give anyone an inheritance. It is not possible through the keeping of the Law to enter into the inheritance of God, the "rest" that we have through faith in Jesus Christ. Joshua, not Moses, led the people into their rest. It is Jesus who gives us rest. He is our Joshua. He has conquered all of our enemies. The last enemy, death, has been conquered by the Lord Jesus. When you know Jesus as your Saviour, you have entered into your inheritance, you are enriched in Him, you have all spiritual blessings through Him. He says, "Come unto me, . . . and I will give you rest" (Matt. 11:28). Jesus Christ is our Joshua—"Jehoshua, Jehovah is salvation."

ZZ–71–72

You may say, "I have never murdered anybody." I'm glad for that, but Jesus said that if you hate someone in your heart, you have committed murder in your heart. We may say, "Well, I have never bowed down before an idol." That may be true, but is Jesus Christ *first* in your life? Are there other gods demanding your allegiance and your obedience? What are you sacrificing to today? It is possible for us to outwardly conform to the standards of the Law but inwardly be committing all kinds of sin. The Law is not only *against* us, but the Law is *contrary* to us.

T–32

Jesus blotted out the handwriting of ordinances that was against us. We are no longer in debt! He has taken it out of the way. The Law is no longer the central thing in our lives. What is the central thing? The cross. Paul said, "God forbid that I should glory except in the cross of our Lord Jesus Christ" (Gal. 6:14 NKJV). Why do we obey God? Because of the Law that is hanging over our head? No. *Because of a life that is within our heart.* Our debt, or responsibility, is not to fulfill the Law. Our debt is to love. Romans 13:8 says, "Owe no man any thing, but to love one another; for he that loveth another hath fulfilled the law." Colossians 2:14 affirms that the bond of indebtedness has been erased and has been nailed to the cross, and therefore, we owe no debt to the Law. Does this mean we are lawless? Of course not! It means that the Law is now written in our

hearts because we have the Holy Spirit within. A new nature within gives us the desire and the power to obey God and to live up to the righteous standards of the Law.

T–33–34

When the Law goes, the flesh has to go because "the strength of sin is the law" (1 Cor. 15:56). When the Law says, "Don't do this!" my old nature says, "I'm going to do it!" When the Law says, "You'd better do that!" I say, "Oh, no I won't!" The old nature *knows* no law, but the new nature *needs* no law. We are not under the bondage of the Law. We were not born as slave children. We were born free. We were born under grace, and therefore, we are no longer under the bondage of the Law.

T–30

Leaders/Leadership

Another area where Satan enters the organization of the church is in the selection of *leaders,* including pastors. It amazes me how few local churches really follow the instructions given in 1 Timothy 3 and Titus 1. Few pastoral selection committees investigate the candidate's testimony with those outside the church, or seek to discover whether or not he has financial honesty and integrity. Too many churches put new Christians into places of leadership, instead of giving them opportunity to mature in areas of lesser ministry.

AAA–123–24

Leaders must learn how to wait. Often their followers don't always see as far as they see or have the faith that they have. The vision of future victory is what motivates a true leader; but, like Israel, too often the people are looking back. I suppose every leader has at one time or another identified with Jesus when He said, "O unbelieving and perverse generation, how long shall I stay with you and put up with you?" (Luke 9:41 NIV).

P–160

The purpose of all ministry is the glory of God and not the aggrandizement of religious leaders or organizations (1 Cor. 10:31; 2 Cor. 4:5). The words of Jesus in His high priestly prayer ought to be the motivating force in all Christian ministry: "I have glorified thee on the earth: I have finished the work which thou gavest me to do" (John 17:4). God has a special task for each of His children (Eph. 2:10); and in the humble, faithful doing of that task, we glorify His name.

G–38

Leadership involves vision, revision, and supervision; but the greatest of these is vision. Leaders must see what others don't see and then challenge others to follow until they do see. "I am doing a great work, so that I cannot come down!" was Nehemiah's testimony (Neh. 6:3), and he never lost that vision.

G–153

In the ministry of the church today, spiritual leaders must constantly ask, "For what does the Scripture say?" (Rom. 4:3 NKJV). God hasn't left us in the dark as to what His church is, how it's to be led, and what it's supposed to do, but if we substitute people's ideas for God's Word, we *will* be in the dark (Isa. 8:20)! Religious novelties and fads abound, creating celebrities and increasing crowds but not always honoring the Lord or building the church. We need leaders, like Moses, who will spend time "on the mount" and find out from the Word what God wants His people to do.

J–32

As never before, our homes, churches, cities, and nations need decisive leaders who will obey the Word of God. "If you ever injected truth into politics," quipped Will Rogers, "you have no politics." The politician asks, "Is it popular?" The diplomat asks, "Is it safe?" But the

97

true leader asks, "Is it God's will? Is it right?"

F–8

While it is true that each member of a local body has an important ministry to perform, it is also true that God has ordained spiritual leaders in the church. I have been privileged to preach in many churches in America, and I have noticed that where the people permit the pastors (elders) to lead, there is usually blessing and growth. I am not talking about high-handed, egotistical dictatorship, but true spiritual leadership. This is God's pattern for the church.

SS–329

Everything in God's work rises and falls with leadership. When God wants to accomplish something, He calls dedicated men and women to challenge His people and lead the way. A decay in the quality of a nation's leaders is an indication that trouble is ahead. The British essayist Walter Savage Landor wrote, "When small men cast long shadows, it's a sign that the sun is setting."

I–17

Legalism

Let no one tell you otherwise: legalism is bondage! Peter called it a "yoke upon the neck" (Acts 15:10). Paul used the same image when he warned the Galatians: "Stand fast therefore in the liberty wherewith Christ hath made us free, and be not entangled again with the yoke of bondage" (Gal. 5:1).

SS–129

If we put ourselves under Law, we forfeit the enjoyment of the blessings of grace (Gal. 5). If we walk in the Spirit, we experience His life-changing power and live so as to please God.

P–105

A legalistic ministry brings death. Preachers who major on rules and regulations keep their congregations under a dark cloud of guilt, and this kills their joy, power, and effective witness for Christ. Christians who are constantly measuring each other, comparing "results," and competing with each other, soon discover that they are depending on the flesh and not the power of the Spirit. There never was a standard that could transform a person's life, and that includes the Ten Commandments. Only the grace of God, ministered by the Spirit of God, can transform lost sinners into living epistles that glorify Jesus Christ.

RR–638

Legalism appeals to the flesh. The flesh loves to be "religious"—to obey laws, to observe holy occasions, even to fast (see Gal. 4:10). Certainly there is nothing wrong with obedience, fasting, or solemn times of spiritual worship, *provided that the Holy Spirit does the motivating and the empowering.* The flesh loves to boast about its religious achievements—how many prayers were offered, or how many gifts were given (see Luke 18:9–14; Phil. 3:1–10).

Another characteristic of religious legalism that fascinates people is the appeal to the senses. Instead of worshiping God "in spirit and in truth" (John 4:24), the legalist invents his own system that satisfies his senses. He cannot walk by faith; he has to walk by sight and hearing and tasting and smelling and feeling. To be sure, true Spirit-led worship does not deny the five senses. We see other believers; we sing and hear the hymns; we taste and feel the elements of the Lord's Supper. But these external things are but windows through which faith perceives the eternal. They are not ends in themselves.

The person who depends on religion can measure himself and compare himself with others. This is another fascination to legalism. But the true believer measures himself with Christ, not other Christians (Eph. 4:11ff). There is no room for pride in the spiritual walk of the Christian who lives by grace; but the legalist constantly boasts about his achievements and his converts (Gal. 6:13–14).

RR–700

Life

We have noted before that *life* is one of the key concepts in John's Gospel. John uses the word at least 36 times. Campbell Morgan has pointed out that mankind needs air, water, and food in order to have life. (We might also add that he needs light.) All of these are provided in Jesus Christ. He provides the "breath" (Spirit) of God (John 3:8; 20:22). He is the Bread of Life (John 6:48) and the Light of Life (John 1:4–5) and He gives us the water of life.

RR–300

The Christian should "love life" (1 Peter 3:10, quoted from Ps. 34:12ff), seeking to put the most into it and getting the most out of it, to the glory of God. We may not enjoy everything in life, or be able to explain everything about life, but that is not important. We live by promises and not by explanations, and we know that our "labor is not in vain in the Lord" (1 Cor. 15:58).

N–38

99

Man's life is a gift from God (Eccles. 3:10). In view of the travail that we experience from day to day, life may seem like a strange gift, but it is God's gift just the same. We "exercise" ourselves in trying to explain life's enigmas, but we don't always succeed. If we believingly accept life as a gift, and thank God for it, we will have a better attitude toward the burdens that come our way. If we grudgingly accept life as a burden, then we will miss the gifts that come our way. Outlook helps to determine outcome.

N–47

The ability to enjoy life comes from within. It is a matter of character and not circumstances. "I have learned, in whatsoever state I am, therewith to be content," Paul wrote to the Philippians (4:11). The Greek word *autarkes,* translated "content," carries the idea of "self-contained, adequate, needing nothing from the outside." Paul carried *within* all the resources needed for facing life courageously and triumphing over difficulties. "I can do all things through Christ who strengthens me" (Phil. 4:13 NKJV).

N–76

Life, Christian

When my wife and I go shopping, I dread going to the yard goods department, but I often have to go because my wife enjoys looking at fabrics. If on the way to the yard goods section I spot the book department, I suddenly come alive! The thing that excites us and "turns us on" is the thing that really is "life" to us. In Paul's case, Christ was his life. Christ excited him and made his life worth living.

SS–70

The Christian life is not a playground; it is a battleground.

SS–70

The Christian life is not a series of ups and downs. It is rather a process of "ins and outs." God works *in,* and we work *out.*

SS–77

Paul was satisfied with Jesus Christ (Phil. 3:10), but he was not satisfied with his Christian life. A sanctified dissatisfaction is the first essential to progress in the Christian race.

SS–88

Wouldn't it be wonderful if Christians put as much determination into their spiritual life as they do their golfing, fishing, or bowling?

SS–90

Life is not a series of accidents; it is a series of appointments. "I will guide thee with mine eye" (Ps. 32:8). Abraham called God "Jehovah-Jireh," meaning "the Lord will see to it" (Gen. 22:14). "And when he putteth forth his own sheep, he goeth before them" (John 10:4). This is the providence of God, a wonderful source of contentment.

SS–97

In the Christian life, knowledge and obedience go together.

SS–109

The most important thing in our Christian lives is not how we look in our own sight, or in the sight of others (1 Cor. 4:1–4)—but how we look in God's sight.

SS–121

The power of Christ in the life of the believer does more than merely restrain the desires of the flesh: *it puts new desires within him.* Nature determines appetite. The Christian has the very nature of God within (2 Peter 1:4).

SS–132

There are some Christians who will defend the truth at the drop of a hat, but their personal lives deny the doctrines they profess to love. "They profess that they know God, but in works they deny him" (Titus 1:16).

SS–133

The Christian life is a "hidden life" as far as the world is concerned, because the world does not know Christ (see 1 John 4:1–6). Our sphere of life is not this earth, but heaven; and the things that attract us and excite us belong to heaven, not to earth. This does not mean that we should ignore our earthly responsibilities. Rather it means that our motives and our strength come from heaven, not earth.

SS–133–34

These four spiritual motivations for godly living impress us with the centrality of Jesus Christ. We forgive because Christ forgave us (Col. 3:13). It is the peace of Christ that should rule in our hearts (Col. 3:15). The Word of Christ should dwell in us richly (Col. 3:16). The name of Christ should be our identification and our authority. "Christ is all, and in all" (Col. 3:11).

SS–141

The most important part of our lives is the part that only God sees, that "inner life" of the soul that nourishes the "outer life" everyone can see. Call it what you will—the devotional life, the "morning watch," the quiet time—the pastor's private life with God is the secret of Christian character, the source of power for service, the lifeline of all that the pastor must be and do.

We must beware of a "religious routine" that is only a pseudo-devotional life: We read the Scriptures, we read a devotional meditation, we go through our prayer list, and we go away no better than we came. No, we go away *worse* than we came because we have fooled ourselves into thinking we have had a spiritual experience with the Lord.

Z–37

It is good to look back to see where we have been and what the Lord has done in us and through us.

As Paul looked back, he saw that life had not always been easy. There had been battles to fight, races to run, stewardship to fulfill. He had fought the world, the flesh, and the devil in city after city, and now he was in his final battle at Rome. There were times when he thought he was going to fail, but the Lord had always brought him through. He could write, "I have fought a good fight."

He could also write, "I have finished my course." This had always been Paul's great desire: "That I might finish my course with joy and the ministry that God has given me. . . ." Each of us has a course to finish. God has a place for each of us to fill and a work for each of us to do. Our times are in His hands. Some are allotted a shorter span for their work; others are given more time. Stephen died as a young man; Paul was permitted to live a longer life. But it is not the length of life that counts—it is the depth and strength of life. Paul had finished his course. He could face the Lord and know that his work had been completed.

TT–19

Light

Light reveals God; light produces fruit; but light also exposes what is wrong.

SS–46

The believer has no business in the darkness. He is a *saint,* which means he is a partaker "of the inheritance of the saints in light" (Col. 1:12). He is a *king,* because he has been delivered "from the power of darkness" and has been translated "into the kingdom of his dear Son" (Col. 1:13). He is "light in the Lord" (Eph. 5:8).

SS–46–47

Loneliness

Loneliness is the malnutrition of the soul that comes from living on

102

substitutes. And the sad thing is, many of the people I meet are *satisfied with substitutes*. They're satisfied with entertainment when God offers them joy. They're satisfied with taking a sleeping pill when God offers them peace. They're satisfied with prices when God offers them values. They're satisfied with fun when God offers them abundant life. They're satisfied playing a role in society when God wants to make them His own children.

EE–10

The root cause of loneliness is the *spiritual* cause. Spiritual relationships are the most important relationships of your life. Life is built on relationships—your relationship to yourself, to others, and to God. Being able to know yourself, accept yourself, and be yourself enables you to relate to others. I have learned that when my relationship to God, to myself, and to others is what it ought to be, loneliness is not a problem.

EE–13

Are you feeling lonely today because of suffering? My word to you is simply this: Jesus Christ is there with you if you've trusted Him as your Saviour. If you know Him as your Lord, you can be encouraged today. "The sufferings of this present time are not worthy to be compared with the glory which shall be revealed in us" (Rom. 8:18). Job said, "I know that my Redeemer lives. I can trust Him, and He will see me through!"

EE–36

Long-Suffering

Along with patience, we need *long-suffering*. This word means "self-restraint" and is the opposite of revenge. Patience has to do primarily with circumstances, while long-suffering has to do with people. God is long-suffering toward people because of His love and grace (2 Peter 3:9). Long-suffering is one fruit of the Spirit (Gal. 5:22). It is among the "grace garments" that the believer should wear (Col. 3:12).

SS–113

Look

Years ago, one of my radio listeners sent me a motto that has often encouraged me: "Look at others, and be distressed. Look at yourself, and be depressed. Look to God, and you'll be blessed!" This may not be a great piece of literature, but it certainly contains great practical theology. When the outlook is bleak, we need the uplook. "Lift up your eyes on high, and behold who hath created these things ... for he is strong in power" (Isa. 40:26).

C–108–9

Lord

"If" (see John 11:21) is the word that hurts, but "Lord" is the word that heals. No matter how broken your heart may be, if you will sincerely give all the pieces to Him and call Him "Lord," He will begin to heal your inner person and put your life together again.

Of course, this means much more than merely saying the word "Lord." It means turning yourself over to Him by faith and trusting Him for today and all of your tomorrows. It means that whenever you find yourself needing special help, you look up to Him and say, "Lord, help me!" When the need has been met, it means looking up and saying, "Thank You, Lord!"

AA–36

Our Lord's exaltation began with His resurrection. When men buried the body of Jesus, that was the last thing any human hands did to Him. From that point on, it was God who worked. Men had done their worst to the Savior, but God exalted Him and honored Him. Men gave Him names of ridicule and slander, but the Father gave Him a glorious name! Just as in His humiliation He was given the name "Jesus" (Matt. 1:21), so in His exaltation He was given the name "Lord" (Phil. 2:11; see Acts 2:32–36).

He arose from the dead and then returned in victory to heaven, ascending to the Father's throne.

His exaltation included sovereign authority over all creatures in heaven, on earth, and under the earth. All will bow to Him (see Isa. 45:23). It is likely that "under the earth" refers to the lost, since God's family is either in heaven or on earth (Eph. 3:14–15). One day all will bow before Him and confess that He is Lord. Of course, it is possible for people to bow and confess *today*, and receive His gift of salvation (Rom. 10:9–10). To bow before Him now means salvation; to bow before Him at the judgment means condemnation.

SS–76

Love

Christian love is "the tie that binds." Love is the evidence of salvation: "We know that we have passed from death unto life, because we love the brethren" (1 John 3:14). It is the "spiritual lubrication" that keeps the machinery of life running smoothly.

SS–65

The fact that we are going to be together in heaven ought to encourage us to love each other on earth.

SS–109

104

There is no place in a Christian's conversation for a know-it-all attitude. While we need to have convictions and not compromise, we must also cultivate a gracious spirit of love. The Christian's *walk* and *talk* must be in harmony with each other.

SS–148

How is it possible for Jesus to *command* us to love one another? Can true love be commanded? You must keep in mind that Christian love is not basically a "feeling"; it is an act of the will. The proof of our love is not in our feelings but in our actions, even to the extent of laying down our lives for Christ and for one another (1 John 3:16). Jesus laid down His life for both His friends and His enemies (Rom. 5:10)! While the emotions are certainly involved, real Christian love is an act of the will. It means treating others the way God treats us.

RR–357–58

Sometimes it's easier to love the sinners than it is to love the saints, as the familiar rhyme puts it:

To live above with saints we love
Will certainly be glory.
To live below with saints we know—
That's another story!

QQ–42

Modern man sees criminals go free when they ought to be condemned, and he has a hard time believing in divine judgment. The overemphasis on the love of God has almost obliterated the doctrine of the holiness of God. Modern man thinks of punishment in terms of reformation, not retribution. It is for the good of the criminal, not for the upholding of the law. God certainly is not less loving than a federal judge!

R–59

What kind of love is the love of God in Jesus Christ? It is a love that seeks and a love that saves. But it is also *a love that keeps.* Listen to Paul's wonderful words of assurance (Rom. 8:38–39).

This is an exciting truth: nothing can separate us from God's love! No matter how difficult the circumstances may be, God's love is still there. What people are and what they do cannot separate us from God's love. Even the very demons from hell and the angels from heaven are helpless to isolate us from God's great love. Nothing in life and nothing in death can come between us and the love of God.

God never turns His back on His children. God never adjusts His love to their conduct. His love is an everlasting love, and a love

105

that never changes, a love that keeps us.

R–97–98

Luxury

What is luxury? The word "luxury" comes from a Latin word that means "excessive." It originally referred to plants that grow abundantly (our English word "luxurious"), but then it came to refer to people who have an abundance of money, time, and comfort, which they use for themselves as they live in aimless leisure. Whenever you are offered "deluxe service," that's the same Latin word: service above and beyond what you really need.

It isn't a sin to be rich or to have the comforts of life, if this is God's will for you. Abraham and David were wealthy men. Yet they used what they had for God's glory. In the eyes of people in the Third World, most of the citizens of the Western world, including the poor, are very wealthy. What the Western world considers necessities are luxuries to the citizens of other nations: things like thermostat-controlled heat and air conditioning, refrigerators, automobiles, adequate medical care, telephones, and abundantly available electricity and fuel.

Luxury doesn't mean owning abundant possessions so much as allowing possessions to own us. To live in luxury is to use what we have only for our own enjoyment and to ignore the needs of others. It means being irresponsible in the way we use our wealth, wasting it on futile pleasures instead of using it for the good of others and the glory of God. A sign in an exclusive clothing store read, "If you must ask the price of our garments, you can't afford them." People who live in luxury don't bother to ask the prices. They don't care how much they spend so long as they get what they want.

E–34–35

M

Marriage

Unless a couple prays together and sincerely seeks God's will in His Word, their marriage begins on a weak foundation.

SS–50

If the husband makes Christ's love for the church the pattern for loving his wife, then he will love her *sacrificially* (Eph. 5:25).

SS–51

The love of the husband for his wife ought to be cleansing her (and him) so that both are becoming more like Christ.

SS–51

The husband's love for his wife should be sacrificial and sanctifying, but it should also be *satisfying* (Eph. 5:28–30).

SS–51

The root of most marital problems is sin, and the root of all sin is selfishness. Submission to Christ and to one another is the only way to overcome selfishness, for when we submit, the Holy Spirit can fill us and enable us to love one another in a sacrificial, sanctifying, satisfying way—the way Christ loves the church.

SS–52

It is God's will that the marriage union be permanent, a lifetime commitment. There is no place in Christian marriage for a "trial marriage," nor is there any room for the "escape hatch" attitude: "If the marriage doesn't work, we can always get a divorce."

For this reason, marriage must be built on something sturdier than good looks, money, romantic excitement, and social acceptance. There must be Christian commitment, character, and maturity. There must be a willingness to grow, to learn from each other, to forgive and forget, to minister to one another. The kind of love Paul described in 1 Corinthians 13 is what is needed to cement two lives together.

RR–593

By going back to the original Edenic Law, Jesus reminded His listeners of the true characteristics of marriage. If we remember these characteristics, we will better know how to build a happy and enduring marriage.

It is a divinely appointed union. God established marriage, and therefore only God can control its character and laws. No court of law can change what God has established.

It is a physical union. The man and woman become "one flesh." While it is important that a husband and wife be of one mind and heart, the basic union in marriage is physical. If a man and woman became "one spirit" in marriage, then death would not dissolve the marriage; for the spirit never dies. Even if a man and woman disagree, are "incompatible," and cannot get along, they are still married, for the union is a physical one.

It is a permanent union. God's original design was that one man and one woman spend one life together. God's original Law knows nothing of "trial marriages." God's Law requires that the husband and wife enter into marriage without reservations.

It is a union between one man and one woman. God did not create two men and one woman, two women and one man, two men, or two women. "Group marriages," "gay marriages," and other variations are contrary to the will of God, no matter what some psychologists and jurists may say.

RR–69

It's a wonderful thing when the covenant community sincerely rejoices with the bride and groom because what they are doing is in the will of God. In my pastoral ministry, I've participated in a few weddings that were anything but joyful. We felt like grieving instead of celebrating. The popular entertainer George Jessel defined marriage as "a mistake every man should make," but the last place you want to make a mistake is at the marriage altar. Contrary to what some people believe, marriage is not "a private affair." This sacred union includes God and God's people, and every bride and groom should want the blessing of God and God's people on their marriage.

D–55

Matter

In the Incarnation, God announced that matter is not evil and

108

that He would use material things as vehicles for revealing Himself and His truth. Christians take a sacramental view of nature, not a gnostic view. The gnostic philosophy is that matter is evil; and the closer you get to the spiritual, the farther you move from the material. The Christian philosophy, however, is that matter is not evil but a gift from God for our benefit and our learning; and the closer you get to God, the more you see His hand in the world around you. The gnostic sees only tree branches waving in the wind, but the Christian sees "the trees of the field clapping their hands" (see Isa. 55:12).

KK–34

Maturity

No one can escape coming into the world as a baby because that is the only way to get here! But it is tragic when a baby fails to mature. No matter how much parents and grandparents love to hold and cuddle a baby, it is their great desire that the baby grow up and enjoy a full life as a mature adult. God has the same desire for His children. That is why He calls to us, "Go on to maturity!" (Heb. 6:1 NIV).

SS–295

While it is true that it is God who "carries us along" to maturity (Heb. 6:1, 3), it is also true that the believer must do his part. We must not be lazy ("slothful," the same word as "dull" in Heb. 5:11) but apply ourselves to the spiritual resources God has given us. We have the promises from God. We should exercise faith and patience and claim these promises for ourselves! Like Caleb and Joshua, we must believe God's promise and want to go in and claim the land! The illustration of the farm (Heb. 6:7–8), and the admonition to be diligent, always remind me of Solomon's warning (Prov. 24:30–34). Read it—*and heed it!*

SS–297–98

Spiritual maturity is one of the greatest needs in churches today. Too many churches are playpens for babies instead of workshops for adults. The members are not mature enough to eat the solid spiritual food that they need, so they have to be fed on milk (Heb. 5:11–14). Just look at the problems James dealt with and you can see that each of them is characteristic of little children:

Impatience in difficulties—
  1:1–4
Talking but not living the
  truth—2:14ff
No control of the tongue—3:1ff
Fighting and coveting—4:1ff

109

Collecting material "toys"—
5:1ff

I am convinced that spiritual immaturity is the number one problem in our churches. God is looking for mature men and women to carry on His work, and sometimes all He can find are little children who cannot even get along with each other.

SS–336

Maturing spiritually means seeing the total work of Christ as it relates to us today, allowing Christ to apply the blessings of His atonement to us personally, and thus becoming more like Him in character and conduct. This involves reading His Word and accepting by faith all that it says about Him and about His people. Paul calls this "reckoning" (Rom. 6:11).

Maturing Christians have an appetite for the solid food of the Word, and they know what Christ is doing for them today as He reigns on the throne. They rejoice in His ministry of making them "complete in every good work to do His will, working in [them] what is well pleasing in His sight" (Heb. 13:21 NKJV); and they are able to share this teaching with others.

K–139

Mediator

Moses was the mediator (go-between) of the Old Covenant in the giving of the Law (Gal. 3:19–20). The people of Israel were so frightened at Mount Sinai that they begged Moses to speak to them so that they would not have to hear God speak (Exod. 20:18–21). Sad to say, this fear of God did not last long; for the people soon disobeyed the very Law they promised to keep. The Mediator of the New Covenant is Jesus Christ, and He is the only Mediator (1 Tim. 2:5). Christ's ministry as Mediator is more excellent than that of the Old Testament priests because it is based on a better covenant; *and His covenant is founded on better promises.*

SS–305

Meditation

Meditation is to the heart and mind what digestion is to the body. Some people read the Bible the way they read a cookbook, and you can starve that way! Take time to let the Spirit reveal Christ to you in the Word. The Holy Spirit is your teacher. If you yield to Him and ask for His help, He will open the Word to you. When you learn a spiritual truth, receive it into your inner self. Make it a part of your "spiritual muscles." As the Lord gradually changes and transforms your mind, you will know Christ better and love Him more.

U–81

What digestion is to the body, meditation is to the soul. As we read the Word and meditate on it, we receive spiritual health and strength for the inner person, and this enables us to obey the will of God.

RR–183

Meekness

When you are meek, you seek nothing for yourself; and when you seek nothing for yourself, God gives you all things. Saul's self-seeking cost him his crown; but David's submission gave him the kingdom. Something else is true: meekness means power under control, and when you can control yourself, everything belongs to you! If you can reign in peace over the kingdom within you, then God will give you all you need in the kingdom without.

DD–91

Meekness is not weakness, for both Moses and Jesus were meek men (Num. 12:3; Matt. 11:29). This word translated "meek" was used by the Greeks to describe a horse that had been broken. It refers to power under control.

RR–21

You and I must make the choice: will we submit in the difficulties of life and cultivate meekness, or will we rebel and produce hardness? The fruit of the Spirit is meekness, but it takes time for the fruit to grow; and the fruit grows best in the storms of life.

DD–89–90

Memory

One problem we face as human beings is the malfunctioning of the memory. Too often we remember what we are supposed to forget, and we forget what we should remember! God says, "Your sins and your iniquities will I remember no more." Yet many Christians go through life shackled with the memory of sins God has already forgotten. Paul wrote, "Forgetting those things which are behind," and yet so many people I meet are still chained to the failures and mistakes of the past. Ask God to give you a poor memory when it comes to the sins of the past that God has already forgiven, buried, and forgotten.

But ask God to give you a good memory when it comes to the help

111

He has given you in the past years of your life.

TT–25

Mercy

God is the Father of mercies because all mercy originates with Him and can be secured only from Him.

God in His grace gives us what we do not deserve, and in His mercy He does not give us what we do deserve. "It is of the LORD's mercies that we are not consumed" (Lam. 3:22). God's mercy is *manifold* (Neh. 9:19), *tender* (Ps. 25:6), and *great* (Num. 14:19). The Bible frequently speaks of the "multitude of God's mercies" so inexhaustible is the supply (Pss. 5:7; 51:1; 69:13, 16; 106:7, 45; Lam. 3:32).

RR–629

Metaphor

It's by using metaphorical language that you turn people's ears into eyes and help them see the truth.

KK–43

Metaphors are something like our Lord's seamless garment: people can even touch the hem of the garment and experience life-changing power.

KK–48

Methods

Often we hear, "I don't care what your method is, just so long as your message is right." But some methods are unworthy of the gospel. They are cheap, whereas the gospel is a costly message that required the death of God's only Son. They are worldly and man centered, whereas the gospel is a divine message centered in God's glory.

SS–164

Mind

When God controls the mind, Satan cannot lead the believer astray.

SS–58

1. Surrender your mind to the Lord at the beginning of each day.
2. Let the Holy Spirit renew your mind through the Word.
3. As you pray, ask God to give you that day a single mind, a submissive mind, a spiritual mind, a secure mind.
4. During the day, "mind your mind!" If you find yourself losing your inner peace and joy, stop and take inventory.
5. Guard the gates of your mind. Remember Paul's admonition in Philippians 4:8: "Whatsoever things are true ... honest ... just

112

. . . pure . . . lovely . . . of good report . . . think on these things."

6. Remember that your joy is not meant to be a selfish thing; it is God's way of glorifying Christ and helping others through you. Jesus first, Others second, Yourself last; and the result is JOY.

SS–99–100

Satan knows the tremendous power of your mind, and he tries to capture it for himself.

AAA–19

Ministry

Ministry is not something we do for God; it is something God does in and through us.

SS–143

You don't earn grace, and you don't deserve grace; you simply receive it as God's loving gift and then share it with others. In ministry, we are channels of God's resources, not reservoirs: "Give, and it will be given to you: good measure, pressed down, shaken together, and running over will be put into your bosom. For with the same measure that you use, it will be measured back to you" (Luke 6:38 NKJV). It's a basic law of the kingdom of God that the servants who know how poor they are be-

come the richest, and those who give the most receive the most and therefore have the most to give.

HH–7

Perhaps that is one of the major differences between Christian ministry and mere humanitarian benevolence, as helpful as it may be. Both can be done in love; both can put food on the table and shoes on the feet; but only true Christian ministry can put grace in the heart so that lives are changed and problems are really solved. The best thing we can do for people is not to solve their problems for them but so relate them to God's grace that they will be enabled to solve their problems and not repeat them.

HH–13

The love that we need for ministry is not a natural ability; it's a supernatural quality that only God can provide.

HH–15

If our motive for serving is anything other than the glory of God, what we do will be only religious activity and not true Christian ministry. We may help people in one way or another, but God will not be able to bless as He wants to do.

HH–19

Miracle, Miracles

Why try to explain away a miracle? What do we prove? Certainly not that we're smarter than God! Either we believe in a God who can do anything, or we must accept a Christian faith that's non-miraculous; and that does away with the inspiration of the Bible, the Virgin Birth, and the bodily resurrection of Jesus Christ. Certainly there's room for honest questions about the *nature* of the miraculous; but for the humble Christian believer, there's never room for questioning the *reality* of the miraculous. C. S. Lewis wrote, "The mind which asks for a nonmiraculous Christianity is a mind in process of relapsing from Christianity into mere 'religion'" (C. S. Lewis, *Miracles* [New York: Macmillan, 1960], 133).

P–116

The greatest miracle of all is the transformation of a lost sinner into a child of God by the grace of God. That is the miracle that meets the greatest need, lasts the longest, and costs the greatest price—the blood of God's Son.

RR–424

"Do you really believe the miracles in the Bible?" a skeptic asked a new Christian who had been a terrible drinker.

"Of course I do!" the believer replied.

The skeptic laughed. "Do you mean that you really believe that Jesus could turn water into wine?" he asked.

"I sure do! In my home He turned wine into food and clothing and furniture!"

RR–698–99

Money

Money wants to claim the loyalty and love that belong only to God, and it has the power to capture us if we're not careful. Money is a marvelous servant but a terrible master, and only a disciplined devotion to God can enable us to keep Mammon in its rightful place.

WW–106

Wealth is something entrusted to us by God, something God doesn't want us to trust. He wants us to trust Him.

WW–106

We must decide what our needs really are and live at that level. We can use whatever extra wealth God sends our way to help meet the needs of others. Simply because we have more income doesn't mean we're obligated to live more expensively, but it does mean we can share more extensively.

WW–110

Wealth can choke the Word of God (Matt. 13:22), create snares and temptations (1 Tim. 6:6–10, 17–19), and give you a false sense of security. People say that money does not satisfy, but it does satisfy *if you want to live on that level.* People who are satisfied only with the things that money can buy are in great danger of losing the things that money cannot buy.

RR–220

Morality

Today, we live in a society that rejects moral absolutes and promotes a "fluid" morality that isn't morality at all. Like the people described in the Book of Judges, everybody is doing what is right in their own eyes (Judg. 21:25). But society's reclassifying of sin hasn't changed anything; God still calls sin an abomination and still judges it.

J–47

Motive

Motive has a great deal to do with ministry. It is possible to do a good thing with a bad motive. The Pharisees prayed, gave offerings, and fasted—all of which were acceptable religious practices—but their motive was to gain the praise of men, not to give glory to God. This robbed them of true and lasting blessing. If I serve you *only* because I am being paid to do it, then I am treating you like a customer, not a person who needs love and care.

EEE–60

Music

It is unfortunate today that we not only have "vain jangling" ("meaningless talk," NIV) in teaching and preaching, but also in music. Far too many songs not only teach *no* doctrine, but many even teach *false* doctrines. A singer has no more right to sing a lie than a teacher has to teach a lie.

SS–211

In the early church, the believers were taught the Word of God and the meanings of basic Christian doctrines. In many churches today, the pulpit and choir loft are places for entertainment, not enlightenment and enrichment.

SS–211

N

Name

What a marvelous planet this will be when Jesus Christ returns to take the government upon His shoulder! But must we wait until then before we can enjoy His reign? No! You and I can turn the government of our lives over to Him today! And when we do, all that is expressed in His names will become real in our own daily experience—"Wonderful, Counselor, Mighty God, Everlasting Father, Prince of Peace."

His name is *Wonderful:* this takes care of the *dullness of life.* No longer must we live on the cheap substitutes of the world in order to have excitement and enjoyment. Jesus Christ makes *everything* wonderful because Wonderful is His name.

His name is *Counselor:* this takes care of the *decisions of life.* The problems of life need perplex and paralyze us no longer, wondering what step to take next. With Jesus Christ as our Counselor, we have the wisdom we need to make the right decisions.

His name is *Mighty God:* this takes care of the *demands of life.* And life *is* demanding! Sometimes we feel like giving up and running off to hide somewhere; but through Jesus Christ, we can face life courageously and have the strength we need to stay on the job and conquer.

His name is *Everlasting Father:* this takes care of the *dimensions of life.* What we are and what we do is part of eternity! A whole new dimension of living is ours through Jesus Christ, when the government of life is on His shoulder.

His name is *Prince of Peace:* this takes care of the *disturbances of life.* In the storms of life, how we long for peace within! What we wouldn't give to have poise and confidence in a threatening world! The answer is Jesus Christ, the Prince of Peace. When He controls the government of your life, He gives you a peace that passes all understanding and explanation.

ZZ–12–13

Names of Jesus

Each name that He bears indicates some blessing He shares.

ZZ–10

Nature, Divine

When the sinner believes on Jesus Christ, the Spirit of God uses the Word of God to impart the life and nature of God within. A baby shares the nature of its parents, and a person born of God shares the divine nature of God. The lost sinner is dead, but the Christian is alive because he shares the divine nature. The lost sinner is decaying because of his corrupt nature, but the Christian can experience a dynamic life of godliness because he has God's divine nature within. Mankind is under the bondage of corruption (Rom. 8:21), but the believer shares the freedom and growth that is a part of possessing the divine nature.

Because we possess this divine nature, we have "completely escaped" the defilement and decay in this present evil world. If we feed the new nature the nourishment of the Word, then we will have little interest in the garbage of the world. But if we "make . . . provision for the flesh" (Rom. 13:14), our sinful nature will lust after the "old sins" (2 Peter 1:9) and we will disobey God. Godly living is the result of cultivating the new nature within.

SS–437

Needs

Did you know that when you trusted Christ as your Savior, you were introduced to eternal sufficiency? Everything you ever need you can get from Jesus Christ. You are rich in Him. He comes to you and says, "What is it you need? Just spell it out to Me. I am Alpha and Omega; I am adequate for every situation; I am sufficient for every need." That is what the grace of God is all about. The grace of God means that God is adequate for every need.

ZZ–42

Certainly God is concerned about your material needs. He feeds the birds of the air and even takes note when a tiny sparrow falls dead to the earth. Second Corinthians 9 deals primarily with a special offering Paul was receiving to assist the poor saints in Jerusalem. Paul assured his readers that their faithful stewardship would result in God's faithful care of their needs. "Because you are faithful to give to others," Paul wrote, "your Lord will be faithful to care for you."

Of course, if a man is careless in his stewardship, he cannot honestly claim this promise. But the Christian who knows how to give to the work of the Lord will find God *giving back to him* in greater measure than ever he gave to others. Christ is sufficient for every material need that a believer faces when he is in the will of God.

CCC–11

Neglect

The usual cause of a dying fire is neglect. That explains why Paul wrote Timothy, "Do not neglect the spiritual gift within you" (1 Tim. 4:14 NASB). If the priest neglected the altar and forgot the daily burnt offering, the fire would go out.

Z–68

Neighbor

A *positive relationship with others* (Prov. 3:27–35) is a blessing the believer enjoys when he or she walks in the wisdom of God. Wise Christians will be generous to their neighbors and live peaceably with them (vv. 27–30), doing their best to avoid unnecessary disagreements (Rom. 12:18). After all, if we truly love God, we will love our neighbor as we would want him to love us.

On the other hand, if our neighbor is a perverse person who scoffs at our faith (Prov. 3:31–35), the Lord will guide us in letting our light shine and His love show so that we will influence him but he won't lead us astray. Sometimes it takes a great deal of patience, prayer, and wisdom to rightly relate to people who don't want Christians in the neighborhood, but perhaps that's why God put us there.

O–41

Neutral

It is tragic to be neutral about Jesus Christ; for, what we believe about Him is a matter of life or death (John 8:24).

RR–331

New Birth

Like physical birth, *spiritual birth involves two parents,* and these two parents are the Spirit of God and the Word of God.

K–3

Obedience

I personally believe that no true Christian can ever be lost, but he will prove the reality of his faith by an obedient life.

SS–45

Sin always robs us; obedience always enriches us.

SS–53

When children obey their parents in the Lord, they will escape a good deal of sin and danger and thus avoid the things that could threaten or shorten their lives.

SS–53

Too many Christians obey God only because of pressure on the outside, and not power on the inside.

SS–78

Practical obedience means pleasing God, serving Him, and getting to know Him better. Any doctrine that isolates the believer from the needs of the world around him is not spiritual doctrine. Evangelist D. L. Moody often said, "Every Bible should be bound in shoe-leather." Paul would agree.

SS–114

Obedience that is not motivated by love cannot produce the spiritual fruit that God wants from His children. If we obey because of fear (God may punish me!) or because of greed (If I obey, God must bless me!), then we cannot expect that close communion with the Father that Jesus promised to those who keep the Word. "If you love Me, you will keep My commandments" (John 14:15 NASB).

XX–66

When our heart's desire is to please our Lord because we love Him, there will be no time for second thoughts or second opinions.

119

Instead, we will echo the words of the Savior: "I delight to do Your will, O my God, and Your law is within my heart" (Ps. 40:8 NKJV).

Which will it be—first-love obedience, or second-opinion disobedience?

W–31

Opinion

No doubt it is wise to get a second opinion in matters medical, but it can be unwise to get a second opinion in matters spiritual. Once God has spoken on a subject, the matter is settled. We can consult no higher source of wisdom, we can appeal to no higher court. "Thus saith the Lord!" is as wise and as high as we can get.

It was Eve's interest in a second opinion that led Adam into sin and, as a result, plunged humanity into sin, death, and condemnation. "You have only heard one side of the story," said Satan, "and what you have heard may not be true. What God has not told you is that this tree can make you wise, and even make you like God." Our first parents fell for the second opinion—and fell.

W–30–31

Orthodoxy

Churches and Christians who defend their orthodoxy but do not pay their bills have no orthodoxy to defend.

SS–178

Outlook

When the outlook is bleak, try the uplook. Apart from God's promises, we have no hope. As Vance Havner used to say, "Faith sees the invisible, chooses the imperishable, and does the impossible." Our work today is a part of God's work in the future, and we want to do our best.

I–81

Outlook determines outcome. If the outlook is selfish, the actions will be devisive and destructive.

SS–74

P

Parents

For the most part, children do not *create* problems; they *reveal* them. Parents who cannot discipline themselves cannot discipline their children. If a father and mother are not *under* authority themselves, they cannot *exercise* authority over others. It is only as parents submit to each other and to the Lord that they can exercise properly balanced spiritual and physical authority over their children.

SS–143

Parents need to listen and be patient as their children talk to them. A listening ear and a loving heart always go together.

SS–143

Past

"Forgetting those things which are behind" does not suggest an impossible feat of mental and psychological gymnastics by which we try to erase the sins and mistakes of the past. *It simply means that we break the power of the past by living for the future.* We cannot change the past, but we can change the *meaning* of the past.

SS–89

Pastor

The pastor who is lazy in his study is a disgrace in the pulpit.

SS–220

Pastors must be peacemakers, not troublemakers. This does not mean they must compromise their convictions, but that they must "disagree" without being "disagreeable." Short tempers do not make for long ministries.

SS–220

A pastor should not be a novice. "Novice" literally means "one newly planted," referring to a young

Christian. Age is no guarantee of maturity, but it is good for a man to give himself time for study and growth before he accepts a church. Some men mature faster than others, of course. Satan enjoys seeing a youthful pastor succeed and get proud; then Satan can tear down all that has been built up.

SS–220

First Timothy 3:4–5 does not mean that a pastor must be married, or, if married, must have children. However, marriage and a family are probably in the will of God for most pastors. If a man's own children cannot obey and respect him, then his church is not likely to respect and obey his leadership. For Christians, the church and the home are one. We should oversee both of them with love, truth, and discipline. The pastor cannot be one thing at home and something else in church. If he is, his children will detect it, and there will be problems. The words "rule" and "ruleth" in 1 Timothy 3:4–5 mean "to preside over, to govern," and suggest that a pastor is the one who directs the business of the church. (Not as a dictator, of course, but as a loving shepherd— 1 Peter 5:3.) The word translated "take care of" in 1 Timothy 3:5 suggests a personal ministry to the needs of the church. It is used in the Parable of the Good Samaritan to describe the care given to the injured man (Luke 10:34–35).

SS–221

The first problem the early church faced was also a modern one: A group of church members was neglected by the ministering staff (Acts 6). I once heard a certain pastor described as "a man who is invisible during the week and incomprehensible on Sunday." Again, somebody in his congregation was feeling neglected.

SS–228

No pastor can lead his people where he has not been himself. "Such as I have, give I thee" is a basic principle of life and ministry (Acts 3:6). The pastor (or church member) who is not growing is actually going backward, for it is impossible to stand still in the Christian life. In his living, teaching, preaching, and leading, the minister must give evidence of spiritual growth.

SS–227

It is tragic when a church keeps its pastors so busy with menial tasks that they have hardly any time for God's Word and prayer (Acts 6:1–7).

SS–225

122

Of course, *every* Christian ought to feed daily on the Word (Jer. 15:16; Matt.4:4; 1 Peter 2:2); but it is especially important that a pastor grow in the Word. It is by daily studying the "good doctrine" and meditating on the Word that he grows in the Lord and is able to lead the church.

The "good minister" preaches the Word that he himself feeds on day by day. But it is not enough to preach the Word; he must also practice it.

SS–225

If pastors are faithful in feeding and leading the people, then the church ought to be faithful and pay them adequately. "Double honor" (1 Tim. 5:17) can be translated "generous pay." (The word *honor* is used as in "honorarium.") It is God's plan that the needs of His servants be met by their local churches; and He will bless churches that are faithful to His servants. If a church is not faithful, and its pastor's needs are not met, it is a poor testimony; and God has ways of dealing with the situation. He can provide through other means, but then the church misses the blessing; or He may move His servant elsewhere.

The other side of the coin is this: A pastor must never minister simply to earn money (see 1 Tim. 3:3). To "negotiate" with churches, or to canvass around looking for a place with a bigger salary is not in the will of God. Nor is it right for a pastor to bring into his sermons his own financial needs, hoping to arouse some support from the finance committee!

SS–232

An elder [pastor] must not be "overbearing" (NIV), a person always pushing to have his own way. While church members ought to respect and follow the leadership of the elders, they should be certain that it is leadership and not dictatorship. A self-willed pastor is arrogant, will not take his people's suggestions and criticisms, and makes sure he always gets his own way.

He must not have a quick temper. There is a righteous anger against sin (Eph. 4:26), but much of our anger is unrighteous and directed against people. A righteous man ought to get angry when wrongs are done. Someone has said, "Temper is such a wonderful thing that it's a shame to lose it." Wise counsel, indeed.

SS–261–62

Patience

We must never think that patience is complacency. Patience is *endurance in action*. It is not the Christian sitting in a rocking chair, waiting for God to do something. It is the soldier on the battlefield, keeping on when the going is tough. It is the runner on the racetrack, refusing to stop because he wants to win the race (Heb. 12:1).

Too many Christians have a tendency to quit when circumstances become difficult. The saintly Dr. V. Raymond Edman, late president of Wheaton College (Illinois), used to remind the students, "It is always too soon to quit."

SS–113

Peace

God's thoughts and plans concerning us come from His heart and lead to His peace. Why look for substitutes?

F–126

Life is full of disturbances. Without are fightings, within are fears. There is no peace. A dozen open doors beckon us to some kind of peace—escape, entertainment, alcohol, sex, dope, hard work—and we run from one door to another hoping to find peace. What we need is Jesus Christ; for His name is Prince of Peace, and that takes care of the disturbances of life.

Y–78

We're prone to want God to change our circumstances, but He wants to change our character. We think that peace comes from the outside in, when in reality it comes from the inside out. Our hearts carry in them their own war or peace, depending on who is in control, Christ or self. Jesus Christ brings peace because He is peace. The more we become like Him, the more we experience His peace and can share it with others.

ZZ–63

The only place you will find peace on earth today is wherever there is a little bit of heaven. There's peace today in heaven, peace purchased by the blood of His cross. There's peace in the hearts of His people who have come to that cross and experienced His salvation. But there will be no peace on earth until He returns and establishes His kingdom. "Of the increase of His government and peace there will be no end, upon the throne of David, and over His kingdom, to order it and establish it with judgment and justice from that time forward, even forever. The zeal of the LORD of hosts will perform this" (Isa. 9:7 NKJV).

ZZ–68–69

Peacemakers

As peacemakers, we must never compromise just to bring about peace. "Peace at any price" is never right in the life of the believer. Peace at the expense of honesty and humility will only lead to more war. The quieting of the surface when the depths are still stormy is no lasting solution to the problem. The false prophets in Ezekiel's day whitewashed the tottering walls and pretended that the situation was in safe hands. "Because, even because they have seduced my people, saying, Peace; and there was no peace; and one built up a wall, and, lo, others daubed it with untempered morter" (Ezek. 13:10). A false peace is more dangerous than an open war, because it gives the impression that the problems have been solved, when in reality the problems have only been covered over. It is honesty, not hypocrisy, that makes for peace. "But the wisdom that is from above is first pure, then peaceable" (James 3:17).

DD–165

Physician

What a wonderful Physician Jesus is! He comes to us in love; He calls us; He saves us when we trust Him; *and He "pays the bill."* His diagnosis is always accurate and His cure is perfect and complete.

RR–188

Pioneer

Jesus is the Pioneer—He wants to lead us into new frontiers. The tragedy is that too many of us as Christians are standing still. Actually, we don't stand still in the Christian life; we either move forward or we go backward. I know the desire of your heart is to go forward in the Christian life. In your praying, in your ministering, in your understanding of the Word of God, in your giving, in all of the outreach of your life, your desire is to go forward and to make progress.

A pioneer has to move into new territory. Some of God's people don't like to move into new territory— they want to keep walking on the same treadmill. But if you want to make progress in your Christian life, then learn what it means to have Jesus Christ as your Pioneer.

ZZ–14

Plan

One of the wonderful things about being a Christian is the knowledge that God has a plan for our lives.

SS–77

Power

God does not trust His power to those who will not trust Him completely.

Y–53

No matter where the Christian may be on this earth, he is seated in the heavenlies with Jesus Christ, and this is the basis of his life and power.

SS–10

If there is to be power in the Christian life, then there must be depth. The roots must go deeper and deeper into the love of Christ.

SS–32

A Christian robbed of power cannot be used of God. "Without me ye can do nothing" (John 15:5).

SS–34

Loss of power in prayer is one of the first indications that we're far from the Lord and need to get right with Him.

A–74

Praise

The believer who prays only to ask for things is missing out on blessings that come with inter-cessions and giving of thanks. In fact, thanksgiving is a great prayer weapon for defeating Satan. "Praise changes things" as much as "prayer changes things."

SS–60

When there is peace in the heart, there will be praise on the lips: "And be ye thankful" (Col. 3:15).

SS–139

In recent years, God's people have been rediscovering the importance of praise. For years, we saw plaques that read PRAYER CHANGES THINGS; but now we see PRAISE CHANGES THINGS. Both are true, because prayer and praise go together. Even when we hurt, in fact, *especially* when we hurt, we need to take our eyes off ourselves and our problems and fix them on the Lord—and praise Him! Praise may not change the circumstances, but it will certainly change *us* and help *us* overcome the circumstances.

GG–31

Prayer

Too many of our prayers focus only on physical and material needs and fail to lay hold of the deeper inner needs of the heart.

SS–31

The Bible nowhere commands any special posture for prayer. Whether we actually bow our knees is not the important thing; that we bow our hearts and wills to the Lord and ask Him for what we need is the vital matter.

SS–31

126

A Christian must "pray always" because he is always subject to temptations and attacks of the devil. A surprise attack has defeated more than one believer who forgot to "pray without ceasing."

SS–60

The third spiritual "tool" that the risen Savior uses to equip his people is prayer: "Our prayer is for your perfection" [katartizo] (2 Cor. 13:9 NIV), Paul wrote. Prayer releases the power of God in our lives and in the lives of others, and this leads to spiritual growth and service. What a blessing, and yet what a battle, it is to pray for God's people!

PP–60–61

Prayer is not our trying to change God's mind. It is learning what is the mind of God and asking accordingly (1 John 5:14–15). The Holy Spirit constantly intercedes for us even though we do not hear His voice (Rom. 8:26–27). He knows the Father's will and He helps us pray in that will.

SS–123

There are times when we simply do not feel like praying—and that is when we must pray the most! The Spirit gives us divine energy for prayer, in spite of the way we feel. The resurrection power of Jesus

Christ is made available to us (Eph. 3:20–21).

SS–123

No Christian has to go through any initiation ceremony to get into the presence of God. We have "boldness to enter into the holiest by the blood of Jesus" (Heb. 10:19). We may "come boldly unto the throne of grace" (Heb. 4:16).

SS–130

The cheap familiarity with which some people approach God in prayer, or talk about Him in testimony or conversation sometimes borders on blasphemy. The saintly Bishop Westcott of Great Britain, author of many scholarly commentaries on various books of the Bible, once wrote: "Every year makes me tremble at the daring with which people speak of spiritual things."

SS–130

God enjoys answering our prayers. But He sometimes delays the answer to increase our faith and devotion and to accomplish His purposes at the right time. God's delays are not always God's denials. As we continue in prayer, our own hearts are prepared for the answer God will give. We find ourselves growing in grace even before His answer comes.

SS–146

Perhaps it is our lack of faith that causes us to pray generally instead of specifically.

SS–146

We must never separate the Word of God from prayer because God has joined them together (Acts 6:4).

SS–146

If church members today put as much concern and enthusiasm into their praying as they did into their baseball games or bowling, we would have revival!

SS–151

Perhaps one reason that revival tarries is because we do not pray fervently for one another.

SS–152

Woe to the congregation whose minister preaches only because it is Sunday and he has to say something! Blessed is that assembly whose pastor can hardly wait to deliver what God has said to his soul. Of course, the fire is lit in the place of prayer and in the study, and then it is taken to the pulpit.

Z–68

If you have only the Word, without prayer, you will have light without heat; but if you have prayer without the Word, you will be in danger of becoming a fanatic—heat without light or "zeal . . . not in accordance with knowledge" (Rom. 10:2 NASB). The important thing in prayer is to yield your will to God's will in the matters that you pray about.

AAA–77

God is still seeking for wall-builders, for intercessors who will plead with God to send revival and renewal to His church. For it's only when God's Spirit is allowed to work among His people that the flood of evil can be stopped and righteousness and justice flourish in the land. The saints want God to judge the wicked, but "the time is come that judgment must begin at the house of God" (1 Peter 4:17).

E–51

"Pray without ceasing" does not mean we must always be mumbling prayers. The word means "constantly recurring," not continuously occurring. We are to "keep the receiver off the hook" and be in touch with God so that our praying is part of a long conversation that is not broken. God knows the desires of the heart (Ps. 37:4), and He responds to those desires even when our voice is silent. See Psalms 10:17, 21:2.

SS–189

When you pray, watch out for both *hasty words* and *too many words* (Matt. 6:7). The secret of acceptable praying is a prepared heart (Ps. 141:1–2), because the mouth speaks what the heart contains (Matt. 12:34–37). If we pray only to impress people, we will not get through to God. The author of *Pilgrim's Progress*, John Bunyan, wrote: "In prayer, it is better to have a heart without words, than words without a heart."

N–65

Prayer is not an emergency measure that we turn to when we have a problem. Real prayer is a part of our constant communion with God and worship of God.

RR–150

The late Peter Deyneka, Sr., my good friend and founder of the Slavic Gospel Association, often reminded me: "Much prayer, much power! No prayer, no power!" Prayer was as much a part of the apostolic ministry as preaching the Word (Acts 6:4). Yet some pastors spend hours preparing their sermons, but never prepare their public prayers. Consequently, their prayers are routine, humdrum, and repetitious. I am not suggesting that a pastor write out every word and read it, but that he think through what he will pray about. This will keep "the pastoral prayer" from becoming dull and a mere repetition of what was "prayed" the previous week.

But the church members also need to be prepared to pray. Our hearts must be right with God and with each other. We must really want to pray, and not pray simply to please people (as did the Pharisees, Matt. 6:5), or to fulfill a religious duty. When a local church ceases to depend on prayer, God ceases to bless its ministry.

SS–214–15

You have probably noticed that "The Lord's Prayer" teaches us to put God's concerns before our own. We pray "Hallowed be Thy Name, Thy kingdom come, Thy will be done" before we bring up our own needs—daily bread, forgiveness, and protection from sin. When our praying centers on the glory of God, we see our needs and requests in proper perspective. Matters that seemed so important have a tendency to shrink to their proper size when measured by the glory of God.

Whatever we pray about, in the will of God and for the glory of God, will be granted by our heavenly Father. When we are available to bring glory to God "on the earth," then God is available to provide what we need.

H–29

Preacher

A preacher is like a man who hears a call for help and drops everything to run to the rescue. He is intent on one thing and he gives himself fully to it. But when he spends five or ten minutes getting into his sermon, he is like a man pausing to visit an art gallery before diving into the ocean to save the drowning swimmer.

VV–75

Preaching must be marked by three elements: conviction, warning, and appeal ("reprove, rebuke, exhort"). To quote an old rule of preachers, "He should afflict the comfortable and comfort the afflicted." If there is conviction but no remedy, we add to people's burdens. And if we encourage those who ought to be rebuked, we are assisting them to sin. Biblical preaching must be balanced.

God's speaker must be patient as he preaches the Word. He will not always see immediate results. He must be patient with those who oppose his preaching. Above all else, *he must preach doctrine.* He must not simply tell Bible stories, relate interesting illustrations, or read a verse and then forget it. *True preaching is the explanation and application of Bible doctrine. Any-thing else is just religious speech-making.*

SS–254

True biblical preaching is the declaration of the Word of God in such a way that men and women see themselves honestly as they are, realize their great need, and turn in fear and trembling to Jesus Christ, the only Physician who can save them.

Y–115

In too many churches today, worship has become entertainment and preaching is merely the happy dispensing of good advice. We need to hear and obey Paul's admonition to Timothy, "Preach the Word" (2 Tim. 4:2). The Holy Spirit is the Spirit of truth (John 16:13) and works by means of the Word of truth (Ps. 119:43; 2 Tim. 2:15). Jeremiah didn't accomplish God's will on earth by means of clever speeches, cunning diplomacy, or skillful psychology. He heard God's Word, took it to heart, and then proclaimed it fearlessly to the people. God did the rest.

F–19

Predestination

Predestination, as it is used in the Bible, refers *primarily* to what God does for saved people. Nowhere in the Bible are we taught that people are predestined to hell, because this word refers only to God's people. The word simply means "to ordain beforehand, to predetermine." Election seems to refer to *people*, while predestination refers to *purposes*.

S–11

Pride

Satan's desire is to work in the local church, to hinder its ministry; and to do this, he must work in and through Christians or professed Christians who are a part of that fellowship. Pride is one of his chief weapons. If he can get a pastor proud of his preaching, a Sunday school teacher proud of his class's growth, or a church officer proud of his experience and leadership, then Satan has a foothold from which to launch his attack. King David brought death and sorrow to Israel simply because he was proud.

AAA–67

Pride opens the door to every other sin, for once we are more concerned with our reputation than our character, there is no end to the things we will do just to make ourselves "look good" before others.

RR–422

Priesthood

Under the Old Covenant, God's people *had* a priesthood; but in the New Covenant, God's people *are* a priesthood. "The priesthood of the believer" is a precious article of the Christian faith, the defense of which has cost many a life. It means that all believers have the same acceptance before God and enjoy equal access to God through Jesus Christ, the Great High Priest.

PP–67

As a "holy priesthood" (1 Peter 2:5), we are set apart for God's exclusive service. As a "royal priesthood" (1 Peter 2:9), we share our Lord's authority, for he is both King and Priest.

PP–70

The very existence of a priesthood in the Old Testament days and a system of sacrifices gave evidence that man is estranged from God. It was an act of grace on God's part that He instituted the whole levitical system. Today, that system is fulfilled in the ministry of Jesus Christ. He is both the sacrifice and the High Priest who ministers to God's people on the basis of His once-for-all offering on the cross.

SS–291

131

Priorities

Priorities are the things that are really important to us in our lives. It is unfortunate that some Christians have their personal priorities confused and, as a result, are hindering the work of Christ. If each believer were practicing Matthew 6:33 "Seek first the kingdom of God . . ." (NKJV), there would be plenty of money for missions, plenty of manpower for service, and the work of the Lord would prosper. But not every Christian is practicing Matthew 6:33.

RR–600

Problems

A change in geography is usually no solution to spiritual problems, because human nature is the same wherever you go, and the enemy is everywhere.

SS–73

Christians who claim to be without problems are either not telling the truth or not growing and experiencing real life. Perhaps they're just not thinking at all. They're living in a religious dream world that has blocked out reality and stifled honest feelings. Like Job's uncomfortable comforters, they mistake shallow optimism for the peace of God and "the good life" for the blessing of God. You never hear them ask what David and Jesus asked: "My God, My God, why hast Thou forsaken Me?" (Ps. 22:1; Matt. 27:46 NASB).

A–109

Ecclesiastes also contains a message for the faithful believer who wants to serve the Lord and have a fulfilled life in Jesus Christ. Solomon says, "Don't bury your head in the sand and pretend that problems don't exist. They do! Face life honestly, but look at life from God's perspective. Man's philosophies will fail you. Use your God-given wisdom, but don't expect to solve every problem or answer every question. The important thing is to obey God's will and enjoy all that He gives you. Remember, death is coming—so, be prepared!"

N–22

Promises

It has been said that God's delays are not always God's denials. As Christians, we don't live on explanations; we live on promises. We know that the Lord is always with us, even if He seems to be ignoring our prayers. "For he hath said, I will never leave thee, nor forsake thee" (Heb. 13:5).

AA–15

No matter how dark the day, the light of God's promises is still shining. No matter how confusing and frightening our circumstances, the character of God remains the same.

You have every reason to trust Him!

E–117

People live by promises, not by explanations.

S–13

We must first be separated from the world and saturated with the Word to be situated by the waters.

JJ-day 3

Prophecy

It is foolish and hurtful to become so obsessed with Bible prophecy that we start to neglect the practical things of the Christian life. Blessed are the balanced!

RR–261

Quench

In using the word *quench* in 1 Thessalonians 5:19, Paul pictured the Spirit of God as fire (see Isa. 4:4; Acts 2:3; Rev. 4:5). Fire speaks of purity, power, light, warmth, and (if necessary) destruction. When the Holy Spirit is at work in our lives and churches, we have a warmth of love in our hearts, light for our minds, and energy for our wills. He "melts us together" so that there is harmony and cooperation; and He purifies us so that we put away sin.

The fire of the Spirit must not go out on the altar of our hearts; we must maintain that devotion to Christ that motivates and energizes our lives.

SS–189

134

R

Rapture

We will not only meet our Lord Jesus Christ at the Rapture, but will also be reunited with our believing friends and loved ones who have died. "Together with them" is a great statement of encouragement. Death is the great separator, but Jesus Christ is the great Reconciler.

SS–181

Nearly twenty centuries have come and gone since our Lord gave the promise of His return, and He has not returned yet. This does not mean that God does not keep His promises. It simply means that God does not follow our calendar. "One day is with the Lord as a thousand years, and a thousand years as one day" (2 Peter 3:8).

SS–183

We must never permit the study of prophecy to become purely academic, or a source of tension or argument. The fact that we will meet our loved ones again and forever be with the Lord is a source of encouragement (1 Thess. 4:18); and the fact that we will not endure God's wrath during the Day of the Lord is another source of encouragement (1 Thess. 5:11).

SS–186

It is the conviction of many students of prophecy that believers in this present age of the church will be raptured by Christ and taken to heaven *before the Tribulation begins* (1 Thess. 4:13–5:11; Rev. 3:10–11). At the close of the Tribulation, they will return to earth with Christ and reign with Him (Rev.

19:11–20:6). I agree with this interpretation, but I do not make it a test of orthodoxy or spirituality.

RR–155

The word *rapture* is not used in this section but that is the literal meaning of "caught up." The Latin word *rapto* means "to seize, to carry off"; and from it we get our English word "rapture."

You and I shall meet the Lord in the air, in person, when He comes for us. The Greek word translated "meet" carries the idea of meeting a royal person or an important person. We have walked with Christ by faith here on earth, but in the air we shall "see Him as He is" and become like Him (1 John 3:1–2 NKJV). What a meeting that will be!

It will be a *glorious* meeting, because we shall have glorified bodies. When He was here on earth, Jesus prayed that we might one day see His glory and share in it (John 17:22–24). The suffering that we endure today will be transformed into glory when He returns (Rom. 8:17–19; 2 Cor. 4:17–18).

It will be an *everlasting* meeting, for we shall be "forever with the Lord." This was His promise: "I will come again, and receive you unto myself; that where I am, there ye may be also" (John 14:3). The goal of redemption is not just to rescue us from judgment, but to relate us to Christ.

Our meeting with the Lord will also be a time of *reckoning*. This is called "the judgment seat of Christ" (Rom. 14:10; 2 Cor. 5:10). The Greek word *bema*, which is translated "judgment seat," referred to the place where the Olympic judges awarded crowns to the winners. Our works will be judged and rewards will be given (1 Cor. 3:8–15).

SS–181

Live expectantly. This does not mean putting on a white sheet and sitting atop a mountain. That is the very attitude God condemned (Acts 1:10–11). But it does mean living in the light of His return, realizing that our works will be judged and that our opportunities for service on earth will end. It means to live "with eternity's values in view."

SS–185

Reckon

The word *reckon* is a translation of a Greek word that is used forty-one times in the New Testament—nineteen times in Romans alone. It appears in Ro-mans 4 where it is translated as "count, reckon, impute." It means "to take into account, to calculate, to estimate." The word *impute*—"to put to one's

136

account"—is perhaps the best translation.

To reckon means "to put to one's account." It simply means to believe that what God says in His Word is really true in your life.

Paul didn't tell his readers to *feel* as if they were dead to sin, or even to *understand* it fully, but to act on God's Word and claim it for themselves. Reckoning is a matter of faith that issues in action. It is like endorsing a check: if we really believe that the money is in the checking account, we will sign our name and collect the money. Reckoning is not claiming a promise, but acting on a fact. God does not command us to become dead to sin. He tells us that we *are* dead to sin and alive unto God, and then commands us to act on it. Even if we do not act on it, the facts are still true.

Paul's first instruction ("know") centered in the *mind,* and this second instruction ("reckon") focuses on the *heart.* His third instruction touches the *will . . . yield.*

RR–531

Regeneration

Regeneration does not simply put us back to where we would have been had Adam never sinned. Regeneration is birth into a brand-new life; it is sharing the very life of God. It is not just a reformation. If regeneration were only reformation, then the next time you sinned, you would have lost it. No, regeneration is that act of God whereby the very life of God is communicated to those who trust Christ as their Savior.

CC–38

Reject

To reject Christ is to reject God, and to reject God is to reject life.

Y–46

It is an awesome thought that the unbeliever will face at the judgment every bit of Scripture he has ever read or heard. The very Word that he rejects becomes his judge! Why? Because the written Word points to the Living Word, Jesus Christ (John 1:14).

Many people reject the truth simply because of the fear of man (John 12:42 43). Among those who will be in hell are "the fearful" (Rev. 21:8). Better to fear God and go to heaven than to fear men and go to hell!

RR–343

Religion

Mere religion can never take away sins or give the sinner a share in eternity. Religion is a part of time; we need a Savior who breaks into time from eternity and who is able to take away our sins. We have such a Savior in Jesus Christ.

Y–60

The word translated "religion" means "the outward practice, the service of a god." It is used only five times in the entire New Testament (James 1:26–27; Acts 26:5; and Col. 2:18, where it is translated "worshiping"). Pure religion has nothing to do with ceremonies, temples, or special days. Pure religion means practicing God's Word and sharing it with others, through speech, service, and separation from the world.

SS–349

Repentance

To seek the Lord means first of all to change our thinking and abandon the vain thoughts that are directing our wayward lives. Disobedient children of God are thinking wrongly about God, sin, and life. They think God will always be there for them to turn to, but He may abandon them to their sins. They think they can sin and get away with it, but they forget that sinners reap what they sow.

E–25

We must distinguish, however, between repentance and remorse and regret. When my consciousness of sin rests only in my mind, then it is regret. When it affects my mind and my heart, it is remorse, and remorse is a dangerous thing. But when my concern over my sin brings me to the place where I am willing to turn from it and obey God—when my concern affects my *will* as well as my mind and my heart—then I have experienced true repentance.

DD–62

True repentance is admitting that what God says is true, and because it is true, to change our mind about our sins and about the Savior.

RR–412

The one thing that encourages us to repent and return to the Lord is the character of God. Knowing that He is indeed "gracious and compassionate, slow to anger and abounding in love" (Joel 2:13 NIV) ought to motivate us to seek His face.

A–55

There is a difference between regret, remorse, and repentance. Regret is a matter of the mind: We are sorry we got caught, and we are sorry that we got into this mess. Remorse is often only a matter of the emotions. We feel terrible about the whole thing. But true repentance is much more than regret and remorse. True repentance involves the whole person. The word "repent" means to change your mind. David had to come to the place where he changed his mind about his sin, about himself, and about God. Repentance begins in the mind, and then it moves into the heart. We feel deeply the awfulness of what we have done. David said, "Against thee, thee only, have I sinned, and done this evil in thy sight" (Ps. 51:4). Did not David sin against Bathsheba? Yes. Did he not sin against Uriah, her husband? Yes. Did he not sin against his own family? Yes, he did, and he paid for it dearly! He sinned against his nation, and there were sad consequences. But in the long run, when we sin against man, we are sinning against God because man is made in the image of God. It is not only that we bring trial and trouble to people; we break the holy law of God and sin against His love and grace.

YY–33–34

Resources

God has not promised to supply all our "greeds." When the child of God is in the will of God, serving for the glory of God, then he will have every need met. Our resources are the providence of God, the power of God, and the promises of God.

SS–99

Rest

One of the key words in this section (Heb. 3:11, 18; 4:1, 3–5, 8–11)

is rest. The writer mentioned two different "rests" found in Old Testament history: (1) *God's Sabbath rest,* when He ceased from His Creation activities (Gen. 2:2; Heb. 4:4); (2) *Israel's rest in Canaan* (Deut. 12:9; Josh. 21:43–45; Heb. 3:11). But he saw in these "rests" illustrations of the spiritual experiences of believers today. The Sabbath rest is a picture of our rest in Christ through salvation (Heb. 4:3; see Matt. 11:28). The Canaan rest is a picture of our present rest as we claim our inheritance in Christ (Heb. 4:11–13; note the emphasis on the Word of God). The first is the rest of salvation; the second is the rest of submission.

But there is a third rest that enters into the discussion, that *future rest* that all believers will enjoy with God. "There remaineth therefore a rest to the people of God" (Heb. 4:9). This word for rest is the Greek work *sabbatismos*—"a keeping of a Sabbath"—and this is the only place in the New Testament where this word is used. When the saints enter heaven, it will be like sharing God's great Sabbath rest, with all labors and battles ended (Rev. 14:13).

SS–287

The Canaan rest for Israel is a picture of the spiritual rest we find in Christ when we surrender to

139

Him. When we come to Christ by faith, we find *salvation* rest (Matt. 11:28). When we yield and learn of Him and obey Him by faith, we enjoy *submission* rest (Matt. 11:29–30). The first is "peace with God" (Rom. 5:1); the second is the "peace of God" (Phil. 4:6–8). It is by believing that we enter into rest (Heb. 4:3); it is by obeying God by faith and surrendering to His will that the rest enters into us.

SS–289

Resurrection

Jesus brought the doctrine of the resurrection out of the shadows and into the light. The Old Testament revelation about death and resurrection is not clear or complete; it is, as it were, "in the shadows." In fact, there are some passages in Psalms and Ecclesiastes that almost make one believe that death is the end and there is no hope beyond the grave. False teachers like to use these passages to support their heretical teachings, but they ignore (or misinterpret) the clear teachings found in the New Testament. After all, it was not David or Solomon who "brought life and immortality to light through the gospel" (2 Tim. 1:10), but Jesus Christ!

By His teaching, His miracles, and His own resurrection, Jesus clearly taught the resurrection of the human body. He has declared once for all that death is real, that there is life after death, and that the body will one day be raised by the power of God.

He transformed this doctrine in a second way: He took it out of a book and put it into a person, Himself. "I am the resurrection and the life" (John 11:25)! While we thank God for what the Bible teaches, we realize that we are saved by the Redeemer, Jesus Christ, and not by a doctrine written in a book. When we know Him by faith, we need not fear the shadow of death.

When you are sick, you want a doctor and not a medical book or a formula. When you are being sued, you want a lawyer and not a law book. Likewise, when you face your last enemy, death, you want the Savior and not a doctrine written in a book. In Jesus Christ, every doctrine is made personal (1 Cor. 1:30). When you belong to Him, you have all that you ever will need in life, death, time, or eternity!

RR–336

The resurrection is an essential part of the gospel message (1 Cor. 15:1–8) and a key doctrine in the Christian faith. It proves that Jesus Christ is the Son of God (Acts 2:32–36; Rom. 1:4) and that His atoning work on the cross has been completed and is effective (Rom.

140

4:24–25). The empty cross and the empty tomb are God's "receipts" telling us that the debt has been paid. Jesus Christ is not only the Saviour, but He is also the Sanctifier (Rom. 6:4–10) and the Intercessor (Rom. 8:34). One day He shall return as Judge (Acts 17:30–31).

RR–387

Riches

It is impossible for the Christian to calculate how rich he is in Christ because the riches of Christ are unsearchable (Eph. 3:8)!

Y–110

Money, self-righteousness, religious works—all of these are cheap substitutes for the true riches we have in Jesus Christ.

Y–108

You do not have to wait until you are an old saint before you can claim your riches in Christ.

SS–11

In Christ, being a Jew or a Gentile is neither an asset nor a liability, for together we share the riches of Christ.

SS–28

We are so rich in Christ that our riches cannot be calculated even with the most sophisticated computer.

SS–33

Right with God

When people are right with God, He leads them in "right paths" (Prov. 4:11), and teaches them "right things" (8:6). Their minds and hearts are filled with right thoughts (12:5), and their lips speak right words (23:16). Their work is right (21:8), because God works in them and through them to accomplish His will (Phil. 2:12–13).

O–128

Rituals

God doesn't want our relationship with Him to be one of shallow, transient feelings and empty words and rituals, hearts that are enthusiastic one day and frigid the next. "For I desired mercy [loyal love], and not sacrifice, and the knowledge of God more than burnt offerings" (Hos. 6:6). A superficial ritual can never take the place of sincere love and faithful obedience (1 Sam. 15:22–23; Amos 5:21–24; Micah 6:6–8; Matt. 9:13; 12:7).

A–28

S

Sacrifice

The fact that Jesus *sat down* after He ascended to the Father is proof that His work was completed (Heb. 1:3, 13; 8:1). The ministry of the priests in the tabernacle and temple was *never done* and *never different:* they offered the same sacrifices day after day. This constant repetition was proof that their sacrifices did not take away sins. What tens of thousands of animal sacrifices could not accomplish, Jesus accomplished with *one sacrifice forever!*

SS–314

I once heard the late Jacob Stam pray, "Lord, the only thing we know about sacrifice is how to spell the word." I wonder if today some of us can even spell the word!

RR–239

Jesus Christ did not need to offer any sacrifices for Himself. On the annual Day of Atonement, the high priest first had to sacrifice for himself; and then he could offer the sacrifices for his nation (Lev. 16). Since Jesus is the sinless Son of God, there was no need for Him to sacrifice for Himself. He was in perfect fellowship with the Father and needed no cleansing.

Our Lord's sacrifice was once and for all, whereas the Old Testament sacrifices had to be repeated. Furthermore, those sacrifices could only *cover* sins; they could never *cleanse* sins. It required the sacrifice of the spotless Lamb of God for sin to be cleansed and removed.

Because He is the sinless, eternal Son of God, and because He offered a perfect sacrifice, Jesus Christ is the "author of eternal salvation" (Heb. 5:9). No Old Testament priest could offer *eternal* salvation to anyone, but that is exactly what we have in Jesus Christ.

SS–293

Saint, Saints

Saints have been saved to the uttermost (Heb. 7:25), but sinners will experience wrath to the uttermost (1 Thess. 2:16).

SS–129

The word *saint* is simply one of the many terms used in the New Testament to describe "one who has trusted Jesus Christ as Saviour." The person is "alive" not only physically, but also spiritually (Eph. 2:1).

SS–9

Salvation

Salvation cannot be "of works" because the work of salvation has already been completed on the cross. This is the work that God does *for* us, and it is a finished work (John 17:1–4; 19:30).

SS–19

God cannot work in us unless He has first worked for us, and we have trusted His Son.

SS–20

There is no such thing in Scripture as the universal fatherhood of God that saves all men. "Ye must be born again" (John 3:7).

SS–31

The whole outlook of a person changes when he trusts Christ, including his values, goals, and interpretation of life.

SS–39

Salvation includes a threefold work:

- the work God does *for* us— salvation;
- the work God does *in* us— sanctification;
- the work God does *through* us—service.

SS–65

You cannot keep silent once you have experienced salvation in Jesus Christ.

SS–107

Any religious teaching that dethrones Jesus Christ, or that makes salvation other than an experience of God's grace through faith, is either confused or anti-Christian and born of Satan.

SS–107

I hear people talking about the life of the Lord Jesus, and we have every reason to appreciate His life, to admire it, to imitate it. But the life of Christ is not what saves lost sinners. Death is coming. Darkness is upon you. You are in spiritual bondage, and the only deliverance there is comes through the blood of the

Lamb. It is not the life of the Lamb or the beauty of the Lamb that saves you but the death of the Lamb.

H–18

We are not saved by continuing in the faith. But we continue in the faith and thus prove that we are saved. It behooves each professing Christian to test his own faith and examine his own heart to be sure he is a child of God (2 Cor. 13:5; 2 Peter 1:10ff).

SS–121

As in 1 Timothy, the title *Saviour* is often repeated in Titus (1:3–4; 2:10, 13; 3:4, 6). The God-given written Word reveals the Saviour, because a Saviour is what sinners need. God's grace brings salvation, not condemnation (Titus 2:11). Jesus could have come to earth as a Judge, but He chose to come as a Saviour (Luke 2:10–11).

SS–260

Salvation involves much more than knowing *facts* about Jesus Christ, or even having special *feelings* toward Jesus Christ. Salvation comes to us when, by an act of the will, we receive Christ as our Saviour and Lord.

EEE–36

Our confidence that we are God's children comes from the wit-

ness of the Word of God before us and the witness of the Spirit of God within us (1 John 5:9–13). However, the assurance of salvation isn't based only on what we know from the Bible or how we feel in our hearts. It's also based on how we live; for if there hasn't been a change in our behavior, then it's doubtful that we've truly been born again (2 Cor. 5:21; James 2:14–26). It isn't enough to say "Lord, Lord!"

P–29

God shows His wisdom by means of the righteousness, sanctification, and redemption that we have in Christ. Each of these theological words carries a special meaning for Christians. *Righteousness* has to do with our standing before God. We are justified: God declares us righteous in Jesus Christ. But we are also *sanctified,* set apart to belong to God and to serve Him. *Redemption* emphasizes the fact that we are set free because Jesus Christ paid the price for us on the cross. This will lead to complete redemption when Christ returns.

So, in one sense, we have the three tenses of salvation given here: we *have been saved* from the penalty of sin (righteousness); we *are being saved* from the power of sin (sanctification); and we *shall be saved* from the presence of sin (redemption). And every believer has all of these blessings in Jesus Christ!

RR–572

Salvation from sin involves much more than a person knowing about Christ, or even having "good feelings" toward Christ. Salvation comes when the sinner commits himself or herself to Jesus Christ and says, "I do!" Then the believer immediately enters into the joys of this spiritual marriage relationship: bearing His name; sharing His wealth and power; enjoying His love and protection; and one day living in His glorious home in heaven. When you are "married to Christ," life becomes a wedding feast, in spite of trials and difficulties.

RR–117

Just as human birth requires two parents, so divine birth has two parents: the Word of God and the Spirit of God. "That which is born of the flesh is flesh; and that which is born of the Spirit is spirit" (John 3:6). "Being born again, not of corruptible seed, but of incorruptible, by the Word of God, which liveth and abideth forever" (1 Peter 1:23). The Spirit of God uses the Word of God to bring about the miracle of the new birth. Since the Word of God is "living and powerful" (Heb.

4:12 NKJV) it can generate life in the heart of the sinner who trusts Christ; and that life is God's life.

SS–345

Sanctify, Sanctification

All saved people are "sanctified in Christ Jesus" (1 Cor. 1:2). Called by His grace, purchased by His blood, and indwelt by His Spirit, we have been set apart from the common things of this world and are devoted to God's exclusive use. The believer's body is the temple of God (1 Cor. 6:19–20); therefore, it is not for rent or for sale. "Present your members [of your body] as slaves to righteousness, resulting in sanctification" (Rom. 6:19 NASB).

XX–108–9

Sanctify simply means "set apart for God's exclusive use." There is *positional* sanctification (Heb. 10:10); we have once and for all been set apart for God. There is also *practical* sanctification (2 Cor. 7:1), a daily dealing with our sins and a growth in holiness. All of this will culminate in *perfect* sanctification (1 John 3:2), when we see Christ and become eternally like Him. Expecting to see Jesus Christ is a great motivation for holy living.

SS–190

Satan

Satan opposes the kingdom by trying to snatch the Word from hearts (Matt. 13:4, 19). But when that fails, he has other ways of attacking God's work. He plants false Christians, he encourages a false growth, and he introduces false doctrine.

RR–45

When there is an unforgiving spirit in a congregation because sin has not been dealt with in a biblical manner, it gives Satan a "beachhead" from which he can operate in the congregation. We grieve the Holy Spirit and "give place to the devil" when we harbor an unforgiving spirit (Eph. 4:27–32).

One of Satan's "devices" is to accuse believers who have sinned so that they feel their case is hopeless. I have had people write me or phone me to ask for help because they have been under satanic oppression and accusation. The Holy Spirit convicts us of sin so that we will confess it and turn to Christ for cleansing; but Satan accuses us of sin so that we will despair and give up.

RR–635

Satan is a liar and tries to get us to listen to his lies, ponder them, and then believe them. This is what he did with Eve. First, he *questioned* God's word ("Yea, hath God said?"), then he *denied* God's word ("Ye shall not surely die!"), and then he *substituted his own lie* ("Ye shall be as gods") (see Gen. 3:1, 4–5).

Satan, of course, is crafty. He knows that believers will not immediately accept a lie, so the enemy has to "bait the hook" and make it easy for us to accept what he has to offer. Basically, Satan is an imitator: he copies what God does and then tries to convince us that his offer is better then God's. How does he do this? By using counterfeit ministers who pretend to serve God, but who are really the servants of Satan.

RR–669

Satan wants us to sacrifice the eternal for the temporary and take the "easy way."

RR–183

Satan can tempt us even in the Holy City at the highest part of the holy temple! Following the example of Jesus, Satan decided to quote Scripture, and he selected Psalm 91:11–12. Of course, he misquoted the promise and besides he omitted "in all thy ways."

RR–183

Beware an empty life! It is a standing invitation for Satan to go to work. In the spiritual war being waged today, you cannot be neutral. You are either for Him or against Him.

FFF–639

Satisfaction

The place of satisfaction is the secret place of the Most High. When you yield to Jesus Christ and link your life with Him, then you find the kind of satisfaction that is worth living for and worth dying for—not the shallow masquerades of this world, but the deep abiding peace and joy that can come only from Jesus Christ.

TT–45

Scorner

Scorners think they know everything, and anybody who tries to teach them is only wasting time. "Proud and haughty scorner [scoffer] is his name" (Prov. 21:24). Scorners can't find wisdom even if they seek for it (14:6), because learning God's truth demands a humble mind and an obedient will. What scorners lack in knowledge they make up for in arrogance. Instead of sensibly discussing a matter with those who could teach them, they only sneer at truth and deny it. My Hebrew lexicons describe them as "frivolous and impudent." Having no intellectual or spiritual ammunition, the scorner depends on ridicule and contempt to fight his enemies.

Scorners show how ignorant they are by the way they respond to advice and reproof. "He who reproves a scoffer gets shame for himself. . . . Do not reprove a scoffer, lest he hate you; rebuke a wise man, and he will love you" (9:7–8 NKJV). "A wise son heeds his father's instruction, but a scoffer does not listen to rebuke" (13:1 NKJV).

O–73

Second Coming

Christians today look for Jesus to return to gather His people to Himself (1 Thess. 4:13–18) and then establish His righteous kingdom. Peter assures us that "the Day of the Lord will come as a thief in the night"; and then, in light of this fact, he asks, "Therefore . . . what manner of persons ought you to be in holy conduct and godliness?" (2 Peter 3:10–11 NKJV). Future hope ought to produce present holiness. Are we ready for His return?

E–106

Security

Our security is in Jesus Christ. When you have trusted Him as your Savior, you have a spiritual security that nothing can destroy. I know, it seems too good to be true; but even salvation itself is too good to be true! Our personal relationship to the Father through Jesus Christ is unchanged and unchangeable, even though our *fellowship* with Him may change from day to day. Our *union* with Christ is secure, no matter what may alter our *communion.*

XX–70

Selfishness

When the enemy fails in his attacks from the *outside,* he then begins to attack from *within;* and one of his favorite weapons is *selfishness.* If he can get us thinking only about ourselves and what we want, then he will win the victory before we realize that he is even at work.

Selfishness means putting myself at the center of everything and insisting on getting what I want when I want it. It means exploiting others so I can be happy and taking advantage of them just so I can have my own way. It is not only wanting my own way but expecting everybody else to want my way too. Why are selfish people so miserable? I think Thomas Merton said it best: "To consider persons and events and situations only in the light of their effect upon myself is to live on the doorstep of hell."

D–59

Sensuality

Sexual sins affect the entire personality. They affect the *emotions,* leading to slavery (1 Cor. 6:12b). It is frightening to see how sensuality can get ahold of a person and defile his entire life, enslaving him to habits that destroy. It also affects a person *physically* (1 Cor. 6:18). The fornicator and adulterer, as well as the homosexual, may forget their sins, *but their sins will not forget them.*

RR–589

Separation

Separation is simply total devotion to God, no matter what the cost. When a man and woman get married, they separate themselves from all other possible mates and give themselves completely to each other. It is total commitment motivated by love, and it is a balanced decision: We separate *from* others *to* the one who is to be our life's mate.

The Jews separated *from* the peoples around them and *to* the Lord and His Word (Neh. 10:28; 9:2). They also united with their brothers and sisters in promising to obey the Law of God (v. 29). Separation that ignores God and other believers is *isolation* and will eventually lead to sin. Only the Holy Spirit can give us the kind of balance we need to live a godly life in this ungodly world. The legalist wants to live by rules, but that style of life only keeps you immature and dependent on your spiritual leaders. The only way to grow in a balanced life is to give yourself totally to God and follow Him by faith.

G–121–22

The important thing is that the honorable vessels not be contaminated by the dishonorable ones. The word "these" (2 Tim. 2:21) refers to the vessels of dishonor (2 Tim. 2:20). Paul is admonishing Timothy to separate himself from false teachers. If he does, then God will honor him, set him apart, and equip him for service. "Useful to the Master" (2 Tim. 2:21 NIV)—what a tremendous honor that is! A useful human vessel of honor does not get involved in the popular things of the world, even the "religious world." He must remain holy, and this means he must be separated from everything that would defile him.

This includes the sins of the flesh as well (2 Tim. 2:22). Paul used a similar admonition in 1 Timothy 6:11–12—"Flee . . . follow . . . fight." True Bible separation is balanced: we flee sin, but we follow after righteousness. If we are not balanced, then we will be isolated instead of separated. In fact, God's man Paul commands us to fellowship "with them that call on the Lord out of a pure heart" (2 Tim. 2:22). After all, this is the purpose of the ministry of the Word (1 Tim. 1:5). It is sad when true believers are isolated because of a false view of separation.

SS–248

Separation without positive growth becomes isolation. We must cultivate these graces of the Spirit in our lives, or else we will be known only for what we oppose rather than for what we propose.

SS–236

Separation must never become isolation (1 Cor. 5:9–10) because God has a work for believers to do in this world (Matt. 5:13–16; John 17:14–18). Jesus was "holy, harmless, undefiled, separate from sinners" (Heb. 7:26); and yet He was the friend of sinners and sought to win them (Luke 15:1–2; Matt. 9:10–11; 11:19). God's people separate from the world so they can be a witness to the world.

I–26

Sermon

A sermon that explains Bible truth but makes no personal and practical application is only a theological lecture. At the same time, a sermon that exhorts and encourages Christian duty, without basing that duty on doctrine, could well be only a piece of religious propaganda. Likewise, a "devotional sermon" that aims only to "warm the heart" will do no lasting good if it has no doctrinal foundation or practical application.

VV–58

It has well been said that nobody goes to church to find out what happened to the Jebusites. A sermon that lingers in the past tense is not really a sermon at all: it is either a Bible story or a lecture. We *live* in the present tense and we need to hear what God has to say to us *today.*

VV–66

Servant

When God wants to accomplish something, He prepares a servant for the task and prepares the task for His servant. The Lord invested seventeen years preparing Joseph for His work in Egypt and eighty years getting Moses ready for forty years of ministry to the people of Israel. David experienced many years of trials and testings before he ascended the throne of Israel. "A prepared servant for a prepared place" is God's approach to ministry.

P–158

The servant's task is not to be popular, but to be obedient. He must feed the family the food that it needs, when it needs it. He should bring out of his "spiritual cupboard" things new and old (Matt. 13:52). Some Bible teachers, in their search for something new and exciting, forget the nutrition of the old truths of the Word. But other ministers are so wrapped up in the old that they fail to discover the new insights and new applications of the old truths. The new grows out of the old, and the old is made more meaningful by the new.

RR–91

A true servant of God does not minister for personal gain; he ministers to help others grow in the faith.

SS–263

Service

God will open up places of service for you as He sees you are ready. Meanwhile, study the Bible and give yourself a chance to grow.

SS–81

150

Obedience and service do not spring from human talent and efforts, but from God's power as we trust Him.

SS–195

It is the Holy Spirit who enables us to serve God, and through Him we can overcome fear and weakness. The word *fear* in 2 Timothy 1:7 means "timidity, cowardice." The Holy Spirit gives us power for witness and for service (Acts 1:8). It is futile for us to try to serve God without the power of the Holy Spirit. Talent, training, and experience cannot take the place of the power of the Spirit.

SS 241

Sex

On hearing the Seventh Commandment, many people in contemporary society smile nonchalantly and ask, "What's wrong with premarital or extramarital sex, or any other kind, for that matter?" After all, they argue, many people indulge in these things and seem to get away with it. Furthermore, these activities are more acceptable today than they were in Solomon's day; why make a big issue out of it? "Life is a game in which the rules are constantly changing," says a contemporary writer; "nothing spoils a game

more than those who take it seriously." So, the verdict's in: sex is fun, so don't take it too seriously.

It's true that some well-known people have indulged in sexual escapades and even bragged about it, including government officials, Hollywood stars, sports heroes, and (alas!) preachers, but that doesn't make it right. Sexual sin is one of the main themes of numerous movies, TV programs, novels, and short stories; yet popularity is no test of right and wrong. Many things that the law says are legal, the Bible says are evil, and there won't be a jury sitting at the White Throne Judgment (Rev. 20:11–15; 21:27; 22:15).

O–47–48

The familiar phrase "apple of your eye" (Prov. 7:2 NIV) refers to the pupil of the eye which the ancients thought was a sphere like an apple. We protect our eyes because they're valuable to us, and so should we honor and protect God's Word by obeying it. Sexual sin often begins with undisciplined eyes and hands (Matt. 5:27–30), but the heart of the problem is . . . the heart (Prov. 7:2–3). If we love God's wisdom as we love those in our family, we wouldn't want to visit the house of the harlot.

O–55

During more than fifty years of ministry, I've listened to many sad stories from people who have indulged in sexual sin and suffered greatly; in almost every instance, the people deliberately put themselves into the place of temptation and danger. Unlike Job, they didn't make "a covenant with [their] eyes not to look lustfully at a girl" (Job 31:1 NIV), nor did they follow the example of Joseph and flee from temptation (Gen. 39:7ff; 2 Tim. 2:22). We can't help being tempted, but we can certainly help tempting ourselves.

O–56

We live in a sex-saturated society. It smiles at monogamous marriages, encourages abortion as a means of birth control, promotes and endorses kinky sex as a means of entertainment, claims that moral absolutes don't exist, and really believes that people can violate moral standards and escape the consequences. Fulton J. Sheen was right when he said, "The Victorians pretended sex did not exist; the moderns pretend that nothing else exists."

There are several reasons why the Lord gives clear instructions concerning personal sexual hygiene, sexual morality, and marriage. For one thing, we're created in the image of God, and the Cre-ator knows what's best for His creation. God certainly wants married couples to enjoy the beautiful gift of sex, but He also wants them to avoid the terrible consequences that come when His laws are violated.

J–80

Sheep

Nowhere in the New Testament do we find an isolated believer. Christians are like sheep; they flock together.

SS–61

Shepherd

If we ministers love the Good Shepherd, we will love His sheep and minister to them in love. If we don't truly love Jesus Christ, then we'll love ourselves and become selfish shepherds who think only of what others can do for us, not what we can do for others.

Church growth experts have determined that one man can effectively pastor only about 150 people; so as the flock grows, the shepherd must enlist help. He must be careful that the people who assist him are true shepherds who are looking for opportunities to serve and not just hirelings looking for jobs. But no matter how large the church becomes, a minister

152

must never lose the shepherd's heart. *Loving the people and maintaining the heart of a servant is the basis for all that the pastor does.*

QQ–35

"Ministry love" isn't something we manufacture. Actors can psych themselves up to play their roles, but shepherds need something deeper to fulfill their calling. Before each performance, the great illusionist Howard Thurston repeated to himself just before the curtain opened, "I love my audience! I love my audience!" That approach may work for magicians, but it won't succeed when it comes to caring for sheep. If the servants of God are to love people, both believers and unbelievers, they must see people as Jesus sees them and respond as He would respond. No amount of psychology can accomplish this; it has to come from the Spirit of God. "God has poured out his love into our hearts by the Holy Spirit, whom he has given us" (Rom. 5:5 NIV).

QQ–39

Signs

As Christian believers today, we are not looking for "signs" of His coming; we are looking for Him!

RR–157

We as believers do not depend on signs; we depend on His unchanging Word, the "sure word of prophecy" (2 Peter 1:19–21).

RR–157

Simple, The

The simple are simple because they reject the truth of God's Word that gives "prudence [common sense] to the simple" (Prov. 1:4 NIV). The tragedy is that simple people actually love their simplicity (v. 22) and have no desire to change. Because they don't take a stand for anything, they fall for everything; this saves them the trouble of thinking, studying, praying, and asking God for wisdom. Instead of working hard to dig into the mines of God's wisdom (2:1–9), the simple prefer to take it easy and pick up whatever cheap trinkets they can find on the surface.

O–72

Sin

Until you and I can remove this terrible thing called sin, we can never move into the marvelous dimension of the eternal. God created us for eternity, and Jesus Christ came to earth to reveal eternity.

Y–57–59

Disease may kill the body, but sin will condemn the soul eternally.

Y–113

Sin has divided mankind, but Christ unites by His Spirit. All believers, regardless of national background, belong to that "holy nation" with citizenship in heaven (Phil. 3:20–21).

SS–25

A Christian is not *sinless,* but he does *sin less*—and less—and less!

SS–45

We would be shocked to see a church member commit some sensual sin, but we will watch him lose his temper in a business meeting and call it "righteous indignation."

SS–135

It's impossible to sin without being bound. One of the deceitful things about sin is that it promises freedom but only brings slavery. "Most assuredly, I say to you, whoever commits sin is a slave of sin" (John 8:34 NKJV). "Do you not know that to whom you present yourselves slaves to obey, you are that one's slaves whom you obey, whether of sin leading to death, or of obedience leading to righteousness?" (Rom. 6:16 NKJV).

O–51

Christians are not people who *are* sinless, but who *do* sin less. The "bent" of their life is toward godliness and obedience.

PP–14

Is there an "unpardonable sin" today? Yes, the final rejection of Jesus Christ. Jesus made it clear that *all* sins can be forgiven (Matt. 12:31). Adultery, murder, blasphemy, and other sins can all be forgiven; they are not unpardonable. But God cannot forgive the rejection of His Son. It is the Spirit who bears witness to Christ (John 15:26) and who convicts the lost sinner (John 16:7–11).

RR–43

Sin, of course, is man's greatest problem. No matter what kind of religion a man has, if it cannot deal with sin, it is of no value. By nature, man is a sinner; and by choice, he proves that his nature is sinful. It has well been said, "We are not sinners because we sin. We sin because we are sinners."

SS–313

The believer has a new relationship to sin. He is "dead to sin." "I am crucified with Christ" (Gal. 2:20). If a drunk dies, he can no longer be tempted by alcohol because his body is dead to all physical senses. He cannot see the alcohol, smell it, taste it, or desire it. In Jesus Christ we have died to sin so that we no longer want to "continue in sin." But we are not only dead to sin; we are also alive in Christ. We have been raised from the dead and now walk in the power of His resurrection. We walk in "newness of life" because we share His life. "I am crucified with Christ: nevertheless I live" (Gal. 2:20).

RR–531

When you read the "tests" for leprosy described in Leviticus 13, you can see how the disease is a picture of sin. Like sin, leprosy is deeper than the skin (Lev. 13:3); it spreads (Lev. 13:5–8); it defiles and isolates (Lev. 13:44–46); and it renders things fit only for the fire (Lev. 13:47–59). Anyone who has never trusted the Saviour is spiritually in worse shape than a leper.

RR–114

The cords of sin get stronger the more we sin, yet sin deceives us into thinking we're free and can quit sinning whenever we please. As the invisible chains of habit are forged, we discover to our horror that we don't have the strength to break them. Millions of people in our world today are in one kind of bondage or another and are seeking for deliverance, but the only One who can set them free is Jesus Christ. "Therefore if the Son makes you free, you shall be free indeed" (John 8:36 NKJV).

O–51–52

It is a *righteous* thing for God to judge sin and condemn sinners. A holy God cannot leave sin unjudged. People who say, "I cannot believe that a loving God would judge sinners and send people to hell" understand neither the holiness of God nor the awfulness of sin. While it is true that "God is love" (1 John 4:8), it is also true that "God is light" (1 John 1:5), and in His holiness He must deal with sin.

A Christian doctor had tried to witness to a very moral woman who belonged to a church that denied the need for salvation and the reality of future judgment. "God loves me too much to condemn me," the patient would reply. "I cannot believe that God would make such a place as a lake of fire."

The woman became ill and the diagnosis was cancer. An operation was necessary. "I wonder if I really should operate," the doctor said to her in her hospital room. "I really love you too much to cut into you and give you pain."

"Doctor," said the patient, "if you really loved me, you would do everything possible to save me. How can you permit this awful thing to remain in my body?"

It was easy then for him to explain that what cancer is to the body, sin is to the world; and both must be dealt with radically and completely. Just as a physician cannot love health without hating disease and dealing with it, so God cannot love righteousness without hating sin and judging it.

SS–194

The scribes and Pharisees saw Matthew and his friends as condemned sinners, but Jesus saw them as spiritually sick "patients" who needed the help of a physician. In fact, He had illustrated this when He cleansed the leper and healed the paralytic. Sin is like a disease: it starts in a small and hidden way; it grows secretly; it saps our strength; and if it is not cured, it kills. It is tragic when sickness kills the body, but it is even more tragic when sin condemns the soul to hell.

RR–194

Sin promises freedom, but it only brings slavery (John 8:34); it promises success, but brings failure; it promises life, but "the wages of sin is death" (Rom. 6:23).

RR–235

There is an "insanity" in sin that seems to paralyze the image of God within us and liberate the "animal" inside. Students of Shakespeare like to contrast two quotations that describe this contradiction in man's nature.

What a piece of work is a man! How noble in reason! how infinite in faculty! in form, in moving, how express and admirable! in action how like an angel! in apprehension how like a god!
    (*Hamlet,* II, ii)

When he is best, he is a little worse than a man; and when he is worst, he is little better than a beast.
    (*The Merchant of Venice,* I, ii)

RR–235

God is no respecter of persons; He must deal with His children when they sin (Col. 3:23–25). A church member criticized her pastor because he was preaching against sin in the lives of Christians. "After all," she said, "sin in the life of a believer is different from sin in the lives of unsaved people." "Yes," replied the pastor, *"it is worse."*

SS–176

There are two extremes to avoid when it comes to dealing with our sins: being too easy on ourselves and being too hard on ourselves.

DD–67

Sin, Unconfessed

When there is unconfessed sin in our lives, nothing we hear sounds good. We attend Sunday school, listen to the Sunday school lesson, and criticize it for being boring. We attend church and criticize: The choir was off-key, the soloist was flat, the pastor's message was too long. Everything we hear is wrong! Do you know why? *We are wrong!* If you have come to the place where everything you hear is wrong, everything you see is wrong, I suggest that maybe *you* are wrong! When David tried to cover his sin, something happened to his ears. He no longer heard the joy of the Lord.

YY–20–21

Singing

While sitting in my backyard one evening, I heard a robin singing merrily from atop a TV aerial. As I listened to him sing, I preached myself a sermon:

> Since early dawn, that bird has done nothing but try to survive. He's been wearing himself out hiding from enemies and looking for food for himself and his little ones. And yet, when he gets to the end of the day, he *sings about it!*
>
> Here I am, created in the image of God and saved by the grace of God, and I complain about even the little annoyances of life. One day, I will be like the Lord Jesus Christ; for that reason alone, I should be singing God's praises just like that robin.

N–29–30

Song

A missionary friend of mine spent 25 years working among the African people of the Congo (now Zaire). When he first traveled up the river to the station where he was going to serve, he was met by the sounds of wailing, moaning, drumbeats, and dismal songs. When my friend left the mission field to return home nearly a quarter of a century later, the people on both sides of the river were singing, "All hail the pow'r of Jesus' name, / Let angels prostrate fall; / Bring forth the royal diadem, / And crown Him Lord of all."

NN–6

Sorrow

Jesus can and does heal the brokenhearted. He identifics with your sorrow because He is "a man of sorrows, and acquainted with grief" (Isa. 53:3). He knows how you feel, and He wants to share His comfort with you. "He healeth the broken in heart, and bindeth up their wounds" (Ps. 147:3).

What should you do so that Jesus can start to heal your broken heart?

The first step is to *accept your sorrow and express it naturally.* God made us to feel pain at the loss of a loved one, and He expects us to express that sorrow. Bereavement is the opportunity God gives us to start the healing process within.

AA–7

God expects us to grieve when loved ones are taken from us. He made us with the ability to sorrow and to weep. Grief is His gift to sorrowing people to help us find healing for our broken hearts. If we refuse to accept His gift, we may later find ourselves with emotional or physical problems.

AA–29

As you experience sorrow and express your grief, be yourself. God made each of us as individuals, and He expects each of us to respond to life in our own individual way. You may have watched your friends go through sorrow in a triumphant manner and yet wonder why your bereavement is so painful. Be yourself—your *best* self—and try not to measure yourself by others.

AA–33

It isn't wrong for Christians to sorrow. It is wrong for Christians to sorrow as those who have no hope.

EE–59

Joy in life is not the absence of sorrow. The Arabs have a motto, "All sunshine makes a desert." If God were to insulate us from sorrow, we would never grow or develop mature character. Heaven is a place of all joy and no sorrow, and hell is a place of all sorrow and no joy. But this present life is a mingling of the two. The fact that Jesus could have joy in the midst of sorrow is proof that we can experience this, too.

H–88

Soul-winning

In our desire to win souls to Christ, we sometimes forget that these souls have bodies, and that often these lives are bruised. Sometimes they have been bruised by other witnesses! It never hurts to take time to pour in the oil and wine. The way to a sinner's heart is often through his bruises.

Y–149

Sovereignty

In these days of almost instant communication and of rapid transportation, when in a matter of minutes nations can come to the brink of war, we forget that God is still sovereign and can do whatever He pleases in the affairs of men. God destroyed everything that the Egyptians trusted—their political unity, their economy, religion, and wisdom—and made them an easy target for the Assyrians. When the international news is frightening and you wonder where God is, read Psalm 2 and Acts 4:23–31; and take hope.

C–52

It is important to remember that divine sovereignty does not negate human responsibility. What God has ordained in eternity must be worked out in time. We may be "chosen . . . from the beginning for salvation," but we are also called through the human instrumentality of the preaching of the gospel (2 Thess. 2:13–14 NASB). The same God who ordains the end (the salvation of lost sinners) also ordains *the means to the end;* and that is where prayer, witnessing, good works, and the exercise of the means of grace all come in.

H–51

The mystery of divine sovereignty and human responsibility will never be solved in this life. Both are taught in the Bible (John 6:37). Both are true, and both are essential.

SS–11

Knowing that the Lord reigns over all things ought to encourage the people of God as we watch world events and grieve over the decay of people and nations. The sovereignty of God isn't an excuse for believers to be indifferent to evil in the world, nor is it an encouragement to slumber carelessly and do nothing. God's ways are hidden and mysterious, and we sometimes wonder why He permits certain things to happen, but we must still pray "Thy will be done" (Matt. 6:10) and then be available to obey whatever He tells us to do.

E–78

Life is something like a doctor's prescription: taken alone, the ingredients might kill you; but properly blended, they bring healing. God is sovereignly in control and has a time and a purpose for everything (Rom. 8:28). This is not fatalism, nor does it rob us of freedom or responsibility. It is the wise providence of a loving Father Who does all things well and promises to make everything work for good.

N–47

What is God's will? The salvation of lost souls, for one thing. If God doesn't want anyone to perish, then why are so many lost? God is long-suffering with lost sinners, even delaying His judgment that they might come to Christ (2 Peter 3:9). But salvation depends on a "knowledge of the truth" (1 Tim. 2:4). Not everyone has heard the truth of the gospel, and many who have heard have rejected it. We

159

cannot explain the mystery of God's sovereignty and man's responsibility (see John 6:37), but realize that both are taught in the Bible and are harmonized in God's great plan of salvation. We do know that prayer is an important part of God's program for reaching a lost world. We have the responsibility of praying for lost souls (Rom. 10:1) and making ourselves available to share the gospel with others.

SS–216

It is possible to be close to people physically and miles away from them spiritually.

SS–64

To be spiritually minded does not require one to be impractical and mystical. Quite the contrary, the spiritual mind makes the believer think more clearly and get things done more efficiently.

To be "spiritually minded" simply means to look at earth from heaven's point of view.

SS–91

The spiritually minded believer is not attracted by the "things" of this world. He makes his decisions on the basis of eternal values and not the passing fads of society. Lot chose the well-watered plain of Jordan because his values were worldly, and ultimately he lost everything. Moses refused the pleasures and treasures of Egypt because he had something infinitely more wonderful to live for (Heb. 11:24–26). "What shall it profit a man, if he shall gain the whole world, and lose his own soul?" (Mark 8:36).

SS–91

When we strive for "spiritual perfection" or "spiritual fullness" by means of formulas, disciplines, or rituals, we go backward instead of forward. Christian believers must beware of mixing their Christian faith with such alluring things as yoga, transcendental meditation, Oriental mysticism, and the like. We must also beware of "deeper life" teachers who offer a system for victory and fullness that bypasses devotion to Jesus Christ. In all things, He must have the preeminence!

SS–104

Spiritual Gifts

No matter what your spiritual gift may be, you are important to the church. In fact, some people who may not have spectacular public ministries are probably just as important behind the scenes as those out in public.

SS–131

160

Steward, Stewardship

Christian stewardship goes beyond paying God a tithe of our income and then using the remainder as we please. True stewardship means that we thank God for *all* that we have (Deut. 8:11–18) and use it as He directs. Giving God 10 percent of our income is a good way to begin our faithful stewardship, but we must remember that God should control what we do with the remaining 90 percent as well.

RR–234–35

Christians are stewards of the *gifts and abilities* God has given them (1 Peter 4:10), and we must use those gifts and abilities to serve others. The thief says, "What's yours is mine—I'll take it!" The selfish man says, "What's mine is mine—I'll keep it!" But the Christian must say, "What's mine is a gift from God—I'll share it!" We are stewards and we must use our abilities to win the lost, encourage the saints, and meet the needs of hurting people.

RR–235

We are stewards of *our time* (Eph. 5:15–17). The phrase "redeeming the time" comes from the business world and means "buying up the opportunity." Time is eternity, minted into precious minutes and handed to us to use either wisely or carelessly.

RR–235

A steward does not own but manages all that his master puts into his hands. Perhaps the most famous steward in the Bible is Joseph, who had complete control over all of Potiphar's business (Gen. 39:1–9). The most important characteristic of a steward is *faithfulness* (Matt. 25:21; 1 Cor. 4:1–2). He must use what his master gives him for the good and glory of his master, and not for himself personally (see Luke 16:1–13).

The elder must never say, "This is mine!" All that he has comes from God (John 3:27) and must be used for God. His time, possessions, ambitions, and talents are all loaned to him by the Lord; and he must be faithful to use them to honor God and build the church. Of course, *all* Christians ought to be faithful stewards, and not the pastors only!

SS–261

A steward owns nothing, but possesses and uses everything that belongs to his master. Joseph was a steward in the household of Potiphar (Gen. 39:1–6). He managed his master's affairs and used all his master's goods to promote his master's welfare. Every steward one day must give an account of his stewardship (Luke 16:1–2). If he is found unfaithful, he will suffer.

SS–163

Submit, Submission

The freedom that Satan offers is really bondage, but the bondage Jesus Christ offers is true freedom. The more we are submitted to Christ, the more we discover and enjoy our freedom.

Y–129

Each person, in submission to the Lord, has no problems submitting to those over him.

SS–56

The test of the submissive mind is not just how much we are willing to take in terms of suffering, but how much we are willing to give in terms of sacrifice.

SS–76

The joy of the submissive mind comes not only from helping others, and sharing in the fellowship of Christ's sufferings (Phil. 3:10), but primarily from the knowledge that we are glorifying God. We are letting our light shine through our good works, and this glorifies the Father in heaven (Matt. 5:16). We may not see the glory today, but we shall see it when Jesus comes and rewards His faithful servants.

SS–77

What does it mean to "submit to God"? It means to stop fighting God and accept His terms of peace (James 4:1–10). It also means to listen to His Word and obey what God says (Job 22:22). A sinner must put away sin (v. 23) and make God his greatest treasure (v. 25); he must pray and seek God's face (v. 27).

M–92

Submission has nothing to do with the *order* of authority, but rather governs the *operation* of authority, how it is given and how it is received.

SS–50

Submission is not subjugation or slavery. Submission is a voluntary surrender to authority, and it's motivated by love and not fear. Subjugated slaves lose their individuality and become pieces of furniture to be bought and sold. However, submitted Christians, yielded to the Lord, develop their individuality and become more like the Master, developing into the kind of people God has planned for them to be. The people who refuse to submit to God's authority will never really discover who they are and what God wants them to do. No matter how successful they may be in the eyes of the world, unless they change they will be failures in the eyes of God.

QQ–49

Success

In the life of the Christian believer, *prosperity* and *success* aren't to be measured by the standards of the world. These blessings are the by-products of a life devoted to God and His Word. If you set out on your own to become prosperous and successful, you may achieve your goal and *live to regret it.* "In whatever man does without God," wrote Scottish novelist George MacDonald, "he must fail miserably, or succeed more miserably." The questions God's people need to ask are: Did we obey the will of God? Were we empowered by the Spirit of God? Did we serve to the glory of God? If we can answer yes to these questions, then our ministry has been successful in God's eyes, no matter what people may think.

P–28

Suffering

The Christian can be joyful even in the midst of pain and suffering.

This kind of joy is not a thermometer but a thermostat.

SS–49

The sacrificial sufferings of Christ are over, but His body, the church, experiences suffering because of its stand for the faith. The Head of the church in heaven feels the sufferings that His people endure. ("Saul, Saul, why persecutest thou me?" [Acts 9:4]) Paul was taking his turn in sharing these afflictions, and others would follow in his train. But Paul did not complain. "For as the sufferings of Christ abound in us, so our consolation also abounds through Christ" (2 Cor. 1:5 NKJV).

SS–121

Satan cannot touch the child of God without the heavenly Father's permission. This is a great encouragement to us, for we know that whatever suffering may come to our lives, God has ordained it and is in complete control. The one thing God will not control is *how we respond to this suffering,* and it is here that Satan can gain his purpose.

AAA–44

This chastening is not always because we have sinned. True, God does "spank" His children if they rebel and refuse to repent. David sinned against God and tried to hide his sin for a year or more. Read Psalm 32 and discover what David suffered physically, emotionally, and spiritually because he would not submit to God. But sometimes God permits suffering in our lives simply to build us up and help us mature.

AAA–45

As believers, we have this confidence: *God is always in complete control.* When God permits Satan to light the furnace, He always keeps His own hand on the thermostat!

AAA–47

Suffering can make us selfish; but when suffering is mixed with grace and faith, it produces love. It is "faith which worketh by love" (Gal. 5:6). When Christians suffer, their faith reaches *upward* to God, and their love reaches *outward* to their fellow believers.

SS–192–93

But we also have hope through *suffering.* He says, "Tribulation worketh patience; and patience, experience; and experience, hope" (Rom. 5:3–4). Suffering makes the unsaved man give up all hope; but when a Christian suffers, he rejoices in hope because he knows that God is in control. The darker the night, the brighter gleam the stars of God's promises.

CCC–39

We can be comforted in our suffering by the knowledge that God is faithfully working out His plan for our good. We see this by His providence, by His presence with us, and by *His provision.* As Joseph cried out to God, the Lord gave him the grace, the patience, and the wisdom that he needed to live through—and grow from—his trials. God had promised to give Joseph a throne, and He kept His promise. Joseph knew that God was going to fulfill everything He had said He would do.

DDD–72

Bad things not only happen to *good* people, but they also happen to a select group of "good people"—*God's* people.

S–21

If we live only for the present and forget the future, trials will make us bitter, not better.

X–23

God always tests us to bring out the best; Satan tempts us to bring out the worst.

X–24

Surety

God does not give us assurance to make us careless. Anyone who is truly born again wants to live a

164

godly life. That is why Jesus is interceding in heaven. We can come to Him at any time and know we are accepted. We can come to Him with any need and know that He will hear us. Just as Judah said, "I will be surety for that lad. I will not come home without him," so Jesus Christ says of us, "I am your surety, and you're going to get home with Me. I'm building a home for you, and you are going to make it because I am your surety."

ZZ–109

Surrender

When you surrender yourself to God, every part of your body belongs to Him and will be protected by Him. He will help you keep your *eyes* from wandering (v. 21), your *neck* from turning your face away from God's path (v. 22; see Luke 9:53), your *feet* walking on the right path (Prov. 3:23, 26), and even your *backbone* safe while you're sleeping (v. 24). If something frightening suddenly happens, you won't be afraid (v. 25; see Pss. 112:7; 121:3–6), because the Lord is protecting you. How we sleep is sometimes evidence of how much we trust the Lord (Pss. 4–5).

O–41

Syncretism

This is an age of "syncretism." People are trying to harmonize and unite many different schools of thought and come up with a superior religion. Our evangelical churches are in danger of diluting the faith in their loving attempt to understand the beliefs of others. Mysticism, legalism, Eastern religions, asceticism, and man-made philosophies are secretly creeping into churches. They are not denying Christ, but they are dethroning Him and robbing Him of His rightful place of preeminence.

SS–105

165

T

Television

Whatever we watch on television, including a religious service, we watch in an entertainment context. No matter what the program is, even a devastating documentary, we don't take it too seriously. Why? Because the world of television is not "real."

Now we can begin to understand why television is a threat to Christian ministry: ministry isn't supposed to be entertainment, and a preacher isn't supposed to be a performer. True ministry implies involvement: we're worshiping in the holy presence of God, and we're obligated to hear God's Word and obey it. When we put religion on TV, a subtle force goes to work that transforms everything. *The viewer does not attend the same service as the people in the sanctuary or in the TV studio.*

WW–99

Temper

I once saw a poster that read, "Temper is such a valuable thing, it is a shame to lose it!" It is temper that helps to give steel its strength. The person who cannot get angry at sin does not have much strength to fight it. James warns us against getting angry at God's Word because it reveals our sins to us. Like the man who broke the mirror because he disliked the image in it, people rebel against God's Word because it tells the truth about them and their sinfulness.

SS–347

Temptation

As God's church today faces enemies and challenges, it is always a temptation to turn to the world or the flesh for help. But our first response must be to examine our hearts to see if there is something we need to confess and make right. Then we must turn to the Lord in faith and obedience and surrender to His will alone. We must trust Him to protect us and fight for us.

C–80

No trial is too great, no temptation is too strong, but that Jesus Christ can give us the mercy and grace that we need, when we need it. "But He is so far away!" we may argue. "And He is the perfect Son of God! What can He know about the problems of weak sinners like us?"

But that is a part of His greatness! When He was ministering on earth in a human body, He experienced all that we experience, *and even more.* After all, a sinless person would feel temptations and trials in a much greater way than you and I could ever feel them. Christ was tempted, yet He did not sin; and He is able to help us when we are tempted. If we fail to hold fast our confession, we are not proving that Jesus Christ has failed. We are only telling the world that *we failed* to draw on His grace and mercy when it was freely available to us.

SS–292

Temptation always carries with it some bait that appeals to our nat-ural desires. The bait not only attracts us, but it also hides the fact that yielding to the desire will eventually bring sorrow and punishment. It is the bait that is the exciting thing. Lot would never have moved toward Sodom had he not seen the well-watered plains of Jordan (Gen. 13:10ff). When David looked on his neighbor's wife, he would never have committed adultery had he seen the tragic consequences: the death of a baby (Bathsheba's son), the murder of a brave soldier (Uriah), the violation of a daughter (Tamar). *The bait keeps us from seeing the consequences of sin.*

SS–342

Testing

Each of us as God's workman will be either *approved* or *ashamed.* The word *approved* means "one who has been tested and found acceptable." The word was used for testing and approving metals. Each trial that we go through forces us to study the Word to find God's will. As we rightly use the Word, we succeed in overcoming our trials, and we are approved by God. Martin Luther once said that prayer, study, and suffering make a pastor; and this is true. We cannot be approved unless we are tested.

SS–247

Thanksgiving

The devil moves in when a Christian starts to complain, but thanksgiving in the Spirit defeats the devil and glorifies the Lord.

SS–50

Thank and *think* also come from the same root word. If we would think more, we would thank more.

SS–50

Giving thanks when everything is falling apart is a real act of faith, but we Christians "walk by faith and not by sight." We say to ourselves, "My Father loves me and knows all about this difficulty. Because He loves me, I can trust Him. He has some wonderful purpose in mind that I cannot see just now. Though He slay me, yet will I trust Him." When you and I express out of faith and love like that, the Father will fill our hearts with His blessing and we will be able to give thanks. It is a miracle of God's grace, and it really works.

Love increases our faith, and when we have faith and love, we will have hope.

TT–31

It has well been said that God's commandments are God's enablements. So, if God commands me to be thankful *for* all things and *in* all things, then He will enable me to obey Him, and I will be a better person because of it.

TT–30

One of my great-uncles was a minister; and he occasionally had Sunday dinner in our home if he happened to be preaching at the church we attended. As a lad, I was impressed by him, especially the way he asked the blessing *after* the meal. Praying *before* the meal was logical and biblical, but why pray after you've finished dessert and coffee? Then I discovered Deuteronomy 8:10, "When you have eaten and are full, then you shall bless the LORD your God for the good land which He has given you" (NKJV). My Uncle Simon took this admonition seriously, and perhaps we should follow his example. If we did, it might keep us from ignoring the Lord while enjoying His blessings. Thanksgiving glorifies God (Ps. 69:30) and is a strong defense against selfishness and idolatry.

B–91

Thinking, Thoughts

Physically, you are what you eat, but spiritually, you are what you think. "As he thinketh in his heart, so is he" (Prov. 23:7). This is why it

168

is important for us as Christians to spend time daily meditating on the Word, praying, and fellowshipping with Christ.

SS–40

Time

"Lord, make me patient!" God will answer that prayer often in ways that will startle us. "And do it right now!" That prayer He cannot answer, for even almighty God must take time to turn clay into useful vessels. The best thing you and I can do is to stop looking at our watches and calendars and simply look by faith into the face of God and let Him have His way— in His time.

W–10

Our "instant" society has so invaded the church that we are constantly looking for shortcuts. All of nature bears witness to the fact that God takes time to accomplish great works, and all of church history, including the Bible, vindicates this witness. It is true that God can, and occasionally does, bring about some great blessing in a short time, but the usual manner of His working is deliberate and at leisure.

I may be wrong, but I have the feeling that we are looking for shortcuts because we don't want to pay the price for doing things God's way. Travail in prayer, hard study, serious heart searching, and patient sowing of the seed have been replaced by methods that guarantee instant results. Results, yes; fruit, no. You cannot have fruit without roots, and you cannot have roots unless you dig deep; and that takes time.

W–15

Take "blessing breaks" during the day. Millions of people take coffee breaks two or three times a day, but very few take time for blessing breaks. What is a blessing break? It is a brief time of praise and prayer for the purpose of quieting the heart and getting new guidance and strength from the Lord. We especially need them when we feel nervous or frustrated or when we feel ourselves getting irritable. Just take a few minutes time to focus on Christ, remember His love, quote a promise, and, by faith, receive the grace needed for that hour. I have done this while in my car waiting for a train to pass, while in line at the supermarket, and even while standing in an elevator in a department store. Believe me, it helps!

W–17

For the unbeliever, time is an enemy; for the dedicated Christian, time is an ally. Jesus Christ entered into time that He might accomplish an eternal purpose. Time became an ally, not an enemy.

Y–62

When I was a young believer, churches often had two-week evangelistic campaigns; and it was not unusual for city-wide meetings to go for a month or six weeks in the summer. Gradually a change took place as "special meetings" were shortened to one week, then to a weekend; and now they are almost obsolete. In my itinerant ministry, more than once I have been reminded to watch the clock so the service could end on time. We live in the age of the digest and fast-food, and this mentality has invaded our churches. We piously sing, "Take Time to Be Holy," but we aren't willing to pay the price to do it.

G–108

Whether we like it or not, it takes time to be holy. Too many of us are caught up in the evangelical rat race, and we simply do not take time to digest the Word of God. We are proud of our libraries, our outlines, our cassettes, and our record of attendance at services and seminars; but are we proud of the results? Are we cultivating a fast-

food faith when we should be taking time to be holy?

W–47

Tithe

A godly deacon said to me once, "If the Old Testament Jew under Law could tithe, how much more ought New Testament Christians under grace!" The New Testament plan for giving is outlined in 2 Corinthians 8–9, but tithing is a good place to start.

We must be careful to give out of the devotion of our hearts, and not as a "bribe" for God's blessings. The late R. G. LeTourneau, well-known Christian manufacturer and philanthropist, used to say, "If you tithe because it pays—it won't pay!"

L–40

Tolerance

The danger. In this day of "pluralism," when society contains people of opposing beliefs and lifestyles, it's easy to get confused and start thinking that *tolerance* is the same as *approval*. It isn't. In a democracy, the law gives people the freedom to worship as they please; and I must exercise patience and tolerance with those who believe and practice things that I feel God has condemned

170

in His Word. The church today doesn't wield the sword (Rom. 13) and therefore it has no authority to eliminate people who disagree with the Christian faith. But we do have the obligation before God to maintain a separate walk so we won't become defiled by those who disagree with us (2 Cor. 6:14–7:1). We must seek by prayer, witness, and loving persuasion to win those to Christ who as yet haven't trusted Him.

B–16–17

Tongue

No matter what may be wrong with us physically, when the doctor examines us, he or she often says, "Stick out your tongue!" This principle applies to the Christian life, for what the tongue does reveals what the heart contains. Inconsistent speech bears witness to a divided heart, for it is "out of the abundance of the heart" that the mouth speaks (Matt. 12:34). "Out of the same mouth proceedeth blessing and cursing," wrote James. "My brethren, these things ought not so to be" (James 3:10).

O–114

Tongues

First Corinthians 14:10 gives us good reason to believe that, when Paul wrote about tongues, he was referring to known languages and not some "heavenly" language. Each language is different and yet each language has its own meaning. No matter how sincere a speaker may be, if I do not understand his language, he cannot communicate with me.

RR–613

When the foundational work of the Apostles and prophets ended, it would seem that the gifts of knowledge, prophecy, and tongues would no longer be needed. "Whether there be tongues, they shall cease" (1 Cor. 13:8). Certainly God could give this gift today if He pleased, but I am not prepared to believe that every instance of tongues is divinely energized. Nor would I go so far as to say that all instances of tongues are either satanic or self-induced.

It is unfortunate when believers make tongues a test of fellowship or spirituality. That in itself would alert me that the Spirit would not be at work. Let's keep our priorities straight and major on winning the lost and building the church.

RR–616

Trials

The trials and testings that come to our lives as Christians are not accidents—they are *appointments.* We must expect to "suffer for His sake" (Phil. 1:29 NKJV). Persecution is not foreign to the believer (1 Peter 4:12ff), but a normal part of the Christian life. We must warn new believers that the way is not easy as they seek to live for Christ; otherwise, when trials come, these babes in Christ will be discouraged and defeated.

SS–172

We are to look not at ourselves, our circumstances, our troubles, or the bumps in the road, but unto Jesus. Yes, the bumps are what you climb on!

TT–12

There is a relationship between our attitude inside and our circumstances outside. If we maintain the proper attitude, God will use our trials to enlarge us. Are you going through a trial today? Give your circumstances to the Lord and trust Him to enlarge you.

JJ–8

In 2 Corinthians 1:5–6, Paul used the word *pathēma,* "suffering," which was also used for the sufferings of our Savior (1 Peter 1:11; 5:1). There are some sufferings that we endure simply because we are human and subject to pain; but there are other sufferings that come because we are God's people and want to serve Him.

We must never think that trouble is an accident. For the believer, everything is a divine appointment. There are only three possible outlooks a person can take when it comes to the trials of life. If our trials are the products of "fate" or "chance," then our only recourse is to give up. Nobody can control fate or chance. If *we* have to control everything ourselves, then the situation is equally as hopeless. But if *God* is in control, and we trust Him, then we can overcome circumstances with His help.

God encourages us in all our tribulations by teaching us from His Word that it is He who permits trials to come.

RR–629

When God puts His children into the furnace, He keeps His hand on the thermostat and His eye on the thermometer (1 Cor. 10:13; 1 Peter 1:6–7).

RR–630

If we are going to turn trials into triumphs, we must obey four imperatives: *count* (James 1:2), *know* (James 1:3), *let* (James 1:4, 9–11), and *ask* (James 1:5–8). Or, to put it another way, there are four essentials for victory in trials: a joyful attitude, an understanding mind, a surrendered will, and a heart that wants to believe.

SS–337

God does not help us by removing the tests, but by making the tests work for us. Satan wants to use the tests to tear us down, but God uses them to build us up.

SS–341

When God sends a trial to us, our first response is usually, *"Why, Lord?"* and then, "Why *me?"* Right away, we want God to give us explanations. Of course, we know that God has reasons for sending tests—perhaps to purify our faith (1 Peter 1:6–9), or perfect our character (James 1:1–4), or even to protect us from sin (2 Cor. 12:7–10)—but we fail to see how these things apply to us. The fact that we ask our Father for explanations suggests that we may not know ourselves as we should or God as we should.

L–110

When trouble comes to our lives, we can do one of three things: endure it, escape it, or enlist it. If we only endure our trials, then trials become our master, and we have a tendency to become hard and bitter. If we try to escape our trials, then we will probably miss the purposes God wants to achieve in our lives. But if we learn to enlist our trials, they will become our servants instead of our masters and work for us; and God will work all things together for our good and His glory (Rom. 8:28).

D–15

Tribulation

Believers do not have to fear future judgment because it is not part of God's appointed plan for us. Will Christians go through the Day of the Lord, that awful period of judgment that God will send on the earth? I think not, and verses like 1 Thessalonians 1:10; 5:9 seem to support this. Christians have always gone through tribulation, since this is a part of dedicated Christian living (John 15:18–27; 16:33). But they will not go through *the* Tribulation that is appointed for the godless world.

I realize that good and godly students of the Word disagree on this matter, and I will not make it a test of fellowship or spirituality. But I do believe that the church will be raptured to heaven prior to the Tribulation period.

SS–185

Trinity

We cannot explain the Trinity. We cannot demonstrate the real-

173

ity of the triune God through the use of mathematics. We know there is one God, but this one God is found in three Persons—God the Father, God the Son, and God the Holy Spirit. They are separate, and yet they are equal. Reginald Heber wrote the song "Holy, Holy, Holy" to commemorate Trinity Sunday on the church calendar. That's why he wrote: "Holy, Holy, Holy! Merciful and Mighty! / God in Three Persons, blessed Trinity!" All three Persons of the Trinity are involved in our salvation. We have been chosen by God the Father, purchased by God the Son, and sealed by God the Holy Spirit. We belong to the triune God.

NN–17

Truth

Truth unites, but lies divide.

BBB–105

God has so arranged things that there is a connection between the facts of the natural world and the *truths* of the spiritual world.

KK–33

Some people hold back the truth because they think this is one way to show love. Others tell the truth but have no love. Jesus Christ is able to blend both truth and love,

and this makes Him an effective Counselor.

Y–35

Understanding the deep truths of God's Word does not give a man a big head; it gives him a broken and contrite heart.

SS–28

Unless we practice the truth, we cannot use the Word of truth.

SS–58

It is one thing to *learn* a truth, but quite another to *receive* it inwardly and make it a part of our inner man (see 1 Thess. 2:13). Facts in the head are not enough; we must also have truths in the heart.

SS–96

God accomplishes His will on earth through *truth;* Satan accomplishes his purposes through *lies.* When the child of God believes God's truth, then the Spirit of God can work in power; for the Holy Spirit is "the Spirit of truth" (John 16:13). But when a person believes a lie, then Satan goes to work in that life; "for he is a liar and the father of lies" (John 8:44 NIV). Faith in God's truth leads to victory; faith in Satan's lies leads to defeat.

AAA–23

One of the evidences that a person is giving the truth of God's Word is that he is rejected. People don't want to hear truth unless they belong to truth (John 10:4).

JJ–27

Learning God's truth and getting it into our heads is one thing, but living God's truth and getting it into our character is quite something else.

RR–531

It is one thing to learn a new spiritual truth, but quite something else to practice that truth in the everyday experiences of life.

Satan does not care how much Bible truth we learn so long as we do not live it. Truth that is only in the head is purely academic and never will get into the heart until it is practiced by the will. "Doing the will of God from the heart" is what God wants from His children (Eph. 6:6). Satan knows that academic truth is not dangerous, but *active* truth is.

RR–201

U

Unbelief, Unbelievers

Faith says, "Yes!" but unbelief says, "No!" Then doubt comes along and says "Yes!" one minute and "No!" the next. It was doubt that made Peter sink in the waves as he was walking to Jesus (Matt. 14:28–31). Jesus asked him, "O thou of little faith, wherefore didst thou doubt?" When Peter started his walk of faith, he kept his eyes on Christ. But when he was distracted by the wind and waves, he ceased to walk by faith; and he began to sink. He was double-minded, and he almost drowned.

Many Christians live like corks on the waves: up one minute, down the next; tossed back and forth. This kind of experience is evidence of immaturity.

SS–340

Paul saw believers and unbelievers in stark contrast to each other: righteousness—un-righteousness, light—darkness, Christ—Belial (Satan), belief—infidelity (unbelief), God's temple—idols. How could you possibly bring these opposites together? The very nature of the Christian demands that he be separated from that which is unholy. When a saved person marries an unsaved partner, it sets up an impossible situation; and the same thing applies to business partnerships and religious "fellowship."

RR–652

The Holy Spirit convicts the world of one particular sin, the sin of *unbelief.* The law of God and the

176

conscience of man will convict the sinner of his *sins* (plural) specifically; but it is the work of the Spirit, through the witness of the believers, to expose the unbelief of the lost world. After all, it is unbelief that condemns the lost sinner (John 3:18–21), not the committing of individual sins. A person could "clean up his life" and quit his or her bad habits and still be lost and go to hell.

RR–362

Understanding

It is not enough for the minister to impart information to people; the people must *receive* it if it is to do them any good. The seed that is received in the good ground is the seed that bears fruit, but this means that there must be an *understanding* of the Word of God (Matt. 13:23). If a believer wants to be edified, he must prepare his heart to receive the Word (1 Thess. 2:13). Not everybody who *listens* really *hears*.

The famous Congregationalist minister, Dr. Joseph Parker, preached at an important meeting and afterward was approached by a man who pointed out an error in the sermon. Parker listened patiently to the man's criticism, and then asked, "And what *else* did you get from the message?" This remark simply withered the critic,

who then disappeared into the crowd. Too often we are quick to judge the sermon instead of allowing the Word of God to judge us.

RR–613

Union

Our union with Christ is a *living* union, so we may bear fruit; a *loving* union, so that we may enjoy Him; and a *lasting* union, so that we need not be afraid.

RR–355

Unity

Unity is not uniformity. Unity comes from within and is a spiritual grace, while uniformity is the result of pressure from without.

SS–35

If we are going to preserve the "unity of the Spirit," we must possess the necessary Christian graces, including humility, meekness, long-suffering, forbearance, endeavor, and peace.

SS–35

We are children in the same family, loving and serving the same Father, so we ought to be able to walk together in unity.

SS–36

Love is evidenced by a *unity of mind* (see Phil. 2:1–11). Unity does

177

not mean uniformity; it means cooperation in the midst of diversity. The members of the body work together in unity, even though they are all different. Christians may differ on *how* things are to be done, but they must agree on *what* is to be done and *why*. A man criticized D. L. Moody's methods of evangelism, and Moody said, "Well, I'm always ready for improvements. What are *your* methods?" The man confessed that he had none! "Then I'll stick to my own," said Moody. Whatever methods we may use, we must seek to honor Christ, win the lost, and build the church. Some methods are definitely not scriptural, but there is plenty of room for variety in the church.

SS–412

What is the basis for true Christian unity? The person and work of Jesus Christ and His glory (John 17:2–5). He has already given His glory to us, and He promises that we will further experience that glory when we get to heaven! All true believers have God's glory within, no matter what they may look like on the outside. Christian harmony is not based on the externals of the flesh but the internals and eternals of the Spirit in the inner person. We must look beyond the elements of our first birth—race, color, abilities, etc.—

and build our fellowship on the essentials of our new birth.

RR–371

Many people today attempt to unite Christians in a way that is not biblical. For example, they will say: "We are not interested in doctrines, but in love. Now, let's forget our doctrines and just love one another!" But Paul did not discuss spiritual unity in the first three chapters of Ephesians; he waited until he had laid the doctrinal foundation. While not all Christians agree on some minor matters of Christian doctrine, they all do agree on the foundation truths of the faith. Unity built on anything other than Bible truth is standing on a very shaky foundation.

SS–38

Spiritual unity is not something we manufacture. It is something we already have in Christ, and we must protect and maintain it. Truth unites, but lies divide. Love unites, but selfishness divides. Therefore, "speaking the truth in love," let us equip one another and edify one another, that all of us may grow up to be more like Christ.

SS–39

Not all unity is good, and not all division is bad. There are times when a servant of God should take a stand against false doctrine and godless practices, and separate himself from them. He must be sure, however, that he acts on the basis of biblical conviction and not because of a personal prejudice or a carnal party spirit.

SS–236

It is better to declare a truce than to wage a war, but the best decision of all is for brethren to "dwell together in unity" (Ps. 133:1). See Ephesians 4:25–32 for directions.

FFF–37

Uttermost

Our Lord's priesthood in heaven is "valid and unalterable." Because it is, we can have confidence in the midst of this shaking, changing world.

What is the conclusion of the matter? It is stated in Hebrews 7:25: "Wherefore [because He is the ever-living, unchanging High Priest], He is able also to save them to the uttermost [completely, forever] that come unto God by Him, seeing He ever liveth to make intercession for them." It is unfortunate that this verse is often read, "He is able to save from the uttermost" instead of "to the uttermost." To be sure, it is true that Christ can save any sinner from any condition; but that is not the import of the verse. The emphasis is on the fact that He saves completely, forever, all who put their faith in Him. Because He is our High Priest forever, He can save forever.

SS–302

V

Values

Living in the future tense means letting Christ arrange the "things" in life according to the proper rank. It means living "with eternity's values in view."

SS–94

God cares for His own (Matt. 10:29–31). It did not cost much to purchase sparrows in the market. If we compare these verses with Luke 12:6, we discover that sparrows were so cheap that the dealer threw in an extra one! Yet the Father knows when a sparrow falls to the ground; *and the Father is there*. If God cares for sparrows in such a marvelous way, will He not also care for His own who are serving Him? He certainly will! To God, we are of greater value than many sparrows.

God is concerned about all of the details of our lives. Even the hairs of our head are numbered— not "counted" in a total, but numbered individually! God sees the sparrow fall to the ground, and God sees when a hair falls from the head of one of His children. When He protects His own, He protects them down to the individual hairs (Luke 21:18). There is no need for us to fear when God is exercising such wonderful care over us.

RR–39

Victories

Before God gives His servants great victories in public, He sometimes prepares them by giving them smaller victories at home. Before David killed the giant Goliath in the

180

sight of two armies, he learned to trust God by killing a lion and a bear in the field where nobody saw it but God (1 Sam. 17:32–37). When we prove that we're faithful with a few things, God will trust us with greater things (Matt. 25:21).

B–53

Victory

As believers, we do not fight *for* victory—we fight *from* victory! The Spirit of God enables us, by faith, to appropriate Christ's victory for ourselves.

SS–57

The Greek goddess of victory was Nike, which also happens to be the name of a United States aerial missile. Both of them are named for the Greek word *nike* (NEE-kay) which simply means victory. But what does victory have to do with maturing love?

Christians live in a real world and are beset with formidable obstacles. It is not *easy* to obey God. It is much easier to drift with the world, disobey Him, and "do your own thing."

But the Christian is "born of God." This means he has the divine nature within him, and it is impossible for this divine nature to disobey God. "For whatever is born of God overcomes the world" (1 John 5:4 NASB). If the old nature

is in control of us, we disobey God; but if the new nature is in control, we obey God. The world appeals to the old nature (1 John 2:15–17) and tries to make God's commandments seem burdensome.

Our *victory* is a result of *faith*, and we grow in faith as we grow in love. The more you love someone, the easier it is to trust him. The more our love for Christ is perfected, the more our faith in Christ is perfected too; because faith and love mature together.

SS–524–25

It's important to remember that the purpose of our Christian armor is not for use in gaining new territory. Of course, we are involved in a conquest. When Jesus said, "The gates of hell shall not prevail against it" (Matt. 16:18), He was talking about the movement of His army, the church, in gaining territory and claiming the spoil. But even as we are conquering, we must remember that we do not fight *for* victory but *from* victory. Christ has already won the victory for us, and we have already entered into our spiritual inheritance in Him. Thus, our role in the battle with the devil is that of claiming and holding on to the territory and inheritance won for us by the Lord Jesus Christ.

GGG–8

Vision, Spiritual

The eyes see what the heart loves. If the heart loves God and is single in this devotion, then the eyes will see God whether others see Him or not. Nothing robs the heart of spiritual vision like sin.

DD–151

W

Wait, Waiting

I confess that *waiting* is one of the most difficult things for me to do, whether it's waiting for a table at a restaurant or waiting for a delayed flight to take off. I'm an activist by nature, and I like to see things happen on time. Perhaps that's why the Lord has often arranged for me to wait. During those times, three phrases from Scripture have encouraged me: "Sit still" (Ruth 3:18), "Stand still" (Exod. 14:13), and "Be still" (Ps. 46:10).

D–49

Waking

When you think of light, you think of waking up to a new day, and Paul presented this picture (Eph. 5:14), paraphrasing Isaiah 60:1. You have the same image in Romans 13:11–13 and 1 Thessalonians 5:1–10. That Easter morning, when Christ arose from the dead, was the dawning of a new day for the world. Christians are not sleeping in sin and death. We have been raised from the dead through faith in Him. The darkness of the graveyard is past, and we are now walking in the light of salvation. Salvation is the beginning of a new day, and we ought to live as those who belong to the light, not to the darkness. "Lazarus, come forth!"

SS–46

Wealth

Too many Christian believers today have limitless wealth at their disposal, and yet they live like paupers.

SS–8

183

Too many Christians have never "read the bank book" to find out the vast spiritual wealth that God has put to their account through Jesus Christ.

SS–14

It is grace that supplies the wealth, but it is faith that lays hold of the wealth. We are saved "by grace . . . through faith" (Eph. 2:8–9), and we live "by grace," through faith (1 Cor. 15:10).

SS–17

The greatest power shortage today is not in our generators or our gas tanks. It is in our personal lives.

SS–17

Wife

A Christian wife who is not doing her job at home gives Satan a beachhead for his operations, and the results are tragic. While there are times when a Christian wife and mother may have to work outside the home, it must not destroy her ministry in the home. The wife who works simply to get luxuries may discover too late that she has lost some necessities. It may be all right to have what money can buy *if* you do not lose what money cannot buy.

How Christian wives and mothers manage their homes can be a testimony to those outside the church. Just as a pastor is to have a good reputation with outsiders (1 Tim. 3:7), and the servants are not to bring reproach on God's Word (1 Tim. 6:1), so the wives are to have a good witness. Women may not be able to be elders of the church, but they can minister for the Lord right in their own homes. (See Titus 2:4–5 for an additional emphasis on this vital ministry.)

SS–230–31

"Keepers at home" does not suggest that a wife's home is a prison where she must be kept! "Caring for the home" is the idea. "Guide the house," Paul wrote (1 Tim. 5:14). The wise husband allows his wife to manage the affairs of the household, for this is her ministry.

SS–263

Every wife will either build the home or tear it down (Prov. 14:1). If she walks with the Lord, she will be a builder; if she disobeys God's wisdom, she will be a destroyer. She must be faithful to her husband, for "A wife of noble character is her husband's crown, but a disgraceful wife is like decay in his bones" (12:4 NIV). A crown or a cancer: What a choice! And beauty isn't the only thing he should look for;

184

it's also important that a wife have wisdom and discretion (11:22).

O-99

Will (Man's)

We must never underestimate the importance of the will in the Christian life. Too many believers have an *intellectual* religion that satisfies the mind but never changes the life. They can discuss the Bible and even argue about it; but when it comes to living it, they fail. Other Christians have an *emotional* religion that is made up of changing feelings. Unless they are on an emotional high, they feel God has forsaken them. God wants *the whole of the inner man* to be devoted to Him: an intelligent mind, a fervent heart, and an obedient will. Our obedience ought to be intelligent, and it ought to be motivated from a warm and loving heart.

AAA-61

Christian living is a matter of the will, not the feelings. I often hear believers say, "I don't feel like reading the Bible." Or, "I don't feel like attending prayer meeting." Children operate on the basis of feeling, but adults operate on the basis of will. *They act because it is right, no matter how they feel.* This explains why immature Christians easily fall into temptation: they let their feelings make the decisions. The more you exercise your will in saying a decisive no to temptation, the more God will take control of your life. "For it is God which worketh in you both to will and to do of his good pleasure" (Phil. 2:13).

SS-343

Will of God

God's will is not given to us for our approval; it is given for our acceptance.

Y-40

God does not give His counsel to the curious or the careless; He reveals His will to the concerned and the consecrated. Some believers take the attitude, "I'll ask God what He wants me to do, and if I like it, I'll do it." The result is predictable: God does not speak to them. Unless we have a serious desire to know and to *do* the counsel of God, He will not reveal His will to us.

Y-39

Christians who are ignorant of God's will lose the enjoyment of God's peace and power. They cannot grow into their full potential, nor can they accomplish what God has planned for them. Instead of

185

traveling first class, they travel second or third class, complaining all the way. They live like paupers because they have cut themselves off from God's great wealth. They spend their lives—even worse, they *waste* their lives—when they could be *investing* their lives.

AAA–27

A business proposition may "look right" to the natural mind, but if it is not based on the truths of God's Word, it will fail. A marriage may seem like "just the right thing" from the human perspective, but if it contradicts the Word of God, it is wrong. In my pastoral ministry, I have seen business deals fail and marriages collapse because they were not done according to the will of God. Somebody believed Satan's lie.

AAA–33

The will of God will never lead you where the grace of God can't keep you and the power of God can't use you. "And who is sufficient for these things? . . . Our sufficiency is of God" (2 Cor. 2:16 and 3:5).

A–86

When a child of God is in the will of God, he can claim the Father's protection and care. But if he willfully gets into trouble and expects God to rescue him, then he is tempting God. (For an example of this, see Exod. 17:1–7.) We tempt God when we "force" Him (or dare Him) to act contrary to His Word. It is a dangerous thing to try God's patience, even though He is indeed long-suffering and gracious.

RR–183

It is better to be hungry *in* the will of God than full *outside* the will of God.

SS–343

If we are practicing true Bible faith, there will be a total response on our part. The mind will know God's will; the emotions will desire to do God's will; and the will itself will respond and obey God's call. I suppose we can call this threefold response perception (the mind), persuasion (the emotions), and performance (the will).

MM–17

When we are seeking to follow the Lord's will, we can be assured that whatever He allows to happen in our lives will be for our ultimate good. He has our best interests at heart. Jeremiah 29:11 tells us, "For I know the thoughts that I think toward you, saith the LORD, thoughts of peace, and not of evil, to give you an expected end." Another translation renders that last phrase, "To give you a future and a hope" (v. 11, NASB). This passage means a great deal to me. It says that God is thinking about us constantly. His plans for us will never be evil. Thus, even in the midst of tears and heartbreak, we can have hope because we know that God will eventually bring some blessing from our sorrow.

DDD–57

The will of God comes from the heart of God (Ps. 33:11), and He delights to make it known to His children *when He knows they are humble and willing to obey*. We don't seek God's will like customers who look at options but like servants who listen for orders. "If any of you really determines to do God's will, then you will certainly know" (John 7:17 TLB) is a basic principle for victorious Christian living. God sees our hearts and knows whether we are really serious about obeying Him. Certainly we ought to use the mind God has given us, but we must heed the warning of Proverbs 3:5–6 and not *lean on* our own understanding.

P–109

Wisdom

Satan often shows up *in the business meetings* of the church too. There is a wisdom from above,

but there is also a wisdom from beneath!

AAA–127

In the language of the New Testament, to be *filled* means to be "controlled by." When we are filled with anger, we are controlled by anger. To be "filled with the Spirit" (Eph. 5:18) means to be "controlled by the Spirit." Paul's prayer, then, is that these believers might be controlled by the full knowledge of God's will.

But how does this take place? How can believers grow in the full knowledge of God's will? Paul's closing words of Colossians 1:9 tell us: "By means of all wisdom and spiritual insight" (literal translation). *We understand the will of God through the Word of God.* The Holy Spirit teaches us as we submit to Him (John 14:26; 16:13). As we pray and sincerely seek God's truth, He gives us through the Spirit the wisdom and insight that we need (Eph. 1:17).

RR–613

If people were as discerning about spiritual things as they are about the weather, they would be better off! The crowd could predict a storm, but it could not foresee the coming judgment. It knew that the temperature was about to change, but it could not interpret the "signs of the times." The Jewish nation had the prophetic Scriptures for centuries and should have known what God was doing, but their religious leaders led them astray.

How tragic that men today can predict the movements of the heavenly bodies, split atoms, and even put men on the moon; but they are blind to what God is doing in the world. They know how to get to the stars, but they do not know how to get to heaven! Our educated world possesses a great deal of scientific knowledge but not much spiritual wisdom.

RR–223

Wise people listen to wise instruction, especially the Word of God. "A wise man will hear, and will increase learning" (Prov. 1:5). Wise people pay attention to spoken instruction as well as to the written Word of God (22:17–21). Jesus warns us to take heed *what* we hear (Mark 4:24) and *how* we hear (Luke 8:18). "Stop listening to instruction, my son, and you will stray from the words of knowledge" (Prov. 19:27 NIV). "Buy the truth, and do not sell it, also wisdom and instruction and understanding" (23:23 NKJV). It costs to acquire wisdom, but it's worth it!

O–62

Wit

The gift of wit is a blessing, but when it is attached to a filthy mind or a base motive, it becomes a curse.

SS–45

Witness, Witnessing

Christians think they are prosecuting attorneys or judges, when God has called all of us to be witnesses.

PP–19

Fathers must live so that they are good examples to their children. Paul could call the Thessalonian believers as witnesses that his life had been exemplary in every way. None of the members of the assembly could accuse Paul of being a poor example. Furthermore, God had witnessed Paul's life; and Paul was not afraid to call God as a witness that he had lived a dedicated life, while caring for the church family.

His life was holy. In the Greek, this means to "carefully fulfill the duties God gives to a person." His life was also righteous. This refers to integrity, uprightness of character, and behavior. This is not the righteousness of the Law but the practical righteousness that God works out in our lives as we yield to Him (Phil. 3:4–10).

Paul's life was also unblamable. Literally, this word means "not able to find fault in." His enemies might accuse him, but no one could level any charge against Paul and prove it. Christians are supposed to be "blameless and harmless" as they live in this world (Phil. 2:15).

SS–166

The angels have never experienced the grace of God, so they can't bear witness as we can. Telling others about the Saviour is a solemn obligation as well as a great privilege, and we who are believers must be faithful.

RR–177

Witnessing is not something that we do for the Lord; it is something that He does through us, *if* we are filled with the Holy Spirit. There is a great difference between a "sales talk" and a Spirit-empowered witness. "People do not come to Christ at the end of an argument," said Vance Havner. "Simon Peter came to Jesus because Andrew went after him with a testimony." We go forth in the authority of His name, in the power of His Spirit, heralding His gospel of His grace.

RR–280–81

Wonder

True wonder captures the whole person; otherwise it is simply novelty or surprise. This is because true wonder is an attitude of life and not an interruption or an isolated event. The person who lives in childlike wonder always lives this way. Wonder is not something he turns on and off like a radio; it is the total outlook of his life at all times.

Y–21

Wonder is a liberating experience; it breaks the shackles and calls us to a life of faith and love.

Y–28

Wonder leads to worship, and worship to growth, and growth to character and service.

Y–27

When life loses its meaning, life loses its wonder. We then become machines!

Y–22

Word of God

The Word of God is the local church's protection and provision, and no amount of entertainment, good fellowship, or other religious substitutes can take its place.

SS–38

189

The more you use a physical sword, the duller it becomes; but using God's Word only makes it sharper in our lives.

SS–59

Society around us is "twisted and distorted," but the Christian stands straight because he measures his life by God's Word, the perfect standard.

SS–78

When we trust God's Word and act on it, then God's power is released in our lives.

SS–79

The Word of God, prayer, and suffering are the three "tools" that God uses in our lives.

SS–79

Our singing must be from our hearts and not just our lips. But if the Word of God is not in our hearts, we cannot sing from our hearts. This shows how important it is to know the Word of God, for it enriches our public and private worship of God.

SS–140

God's Word does not have to be edited or changed to meet different problems in various situations, for it is always applicable.

SS–153

A believer who understands the Word will have a burning heart, not a big head (Luke 24:32; and see Dan. 9:1–20).

SS–234

When you know Jesus Christ as your Savior, the Word of God becomes your mirror, according to 2 Corinthians 3:18: "But we all, with [unveiled] face beholding as in a [mirror] the glory of the Lord, are changed into the same image from glory to glory, even as by the Spirit of the Lord." When the child of God looks into the Word of God (the mirror) and sees the Son of God, he is transformed by the Spirit of God into the image of God for the glory of God. The Law never changed anybody; it is only a mirror that shows us our sin. When you have Jesus Christ as your Saviour and the Holy Spirit lives within you, the Word becomes a mirror that transforms you from glory to glory. You become more like the Lord Jesus Christ! If you put yourself under the Law, all you can do is look in the mirror and see how dirty you are. That creates guilt and condemnation, but it never changes you for the better. It always changes you for the worse.

T–36–37

When we believe God's Word and obey, He releases power—

190

divine energy—that works in our lives to fulfill His purposes. The Word of God within us is a great source of power in times of testing and suffering. If we appreciate the Word (the heart), appropriate the Word (the mind), and apply the Word (the will), then the whole person will be controlled by God's Word and He will give us the victory.

SS–169

Now, I'm not one of those superstitious persons who seeks God's direction by opening my Bible just anywhere and pointing to a verse. But when the Spirit of God impresses me with a passage *in the course of my regular Bible reading,* I stop and pay attention. I don't read my Bible in the past tense. Our God is the God of the living, who dwells in the eternal present; and I believe He wants to communicate with me each day through His Word. God not only has a special plan for my life, but He wants to reveal that plan to me and help me fulfill it.

HH–37

The theme of Hebrews seems to be: "God has spoken; we have His Word. What are we doing about it?"

SS–277

If we are to use God's mirror profitably, then we must gaze into it carefully and with serious intent (James 1:25.) No quick glances will do. We must examine our own hearts and lives in the light of God's Word. This requires time, attention, and sincere devotion. Five minutes with God each day will never accomplish a deep spiritual examination.

I have been fortunate with the doctors who have cared for me through the years, and I owe a great deal to them. Each of them has possessed two qualities that I have appreciated: they have spent time with me and have not been in a hurry, and they have always told me the truth. When Jesus, the Great Physician (Matt. 9:12), examines us, He uses His Word; and He wants us to give Him sufficient time to do the job well. Perhaps one reason we glance into the Word instead of gaze into the Word is that we are afraid of what we might see.

After seeing ourselves, we must remember what we are and what God says, and we must *do the Word.* The blessing comes in the doing, not in the reading of the Word. "This man shall be blessed in his doing" (James 1:25, literal translation). The emphasis in James is on the practice of the Word. We are to *continue* after reading the Word (James 1:25; see

Acts 1:14; 2:42, 46; 13:43; 14:22; 26:22 for examples of this in the early church).

SS–348

Of course, merely *reading* your Bible will not nourish you, any more than reading a cookbook or a restaurant menu will feed a starving man. You must make the Word a part of your inner life by understanding it, meditating on it, memorizing it, and obeying it. Only then will you grow in the inner man and be strong because the Word is abiding in you (1 John 2:14).

CCC–17

You can never exaggerate the importance of the Christian soldier spending time daily in the Word of God. Unless daily we take the sword of the Spirit by faith (Eph. 6:17), we go into the battle unarmed and therefore unprepared. Spiritually minded believers are victorious because they allow the Word of God to "saturate" their minds and hearts. The Spirit using the Word controls their desires and decisions and this is the secret of victory.

P–97

Many times we have seen the Word of God quiet hearts in a wonderful way. The sensitive pastor will use Scripture as medicine to heal

(Ps. 107:20) and as light to overcome the darkness. He will trust the Spirit of God to apply the Word to hearts in His own way. The beautiful thing about Scripture is that it meets the need without violating the personality. A promise from God will calm the heart and yet will permit the person to weep and express normal grief. "Joy in the midst of sorrow" is often the believer's experience.

R–31

Words

The phrase "idle word" in Matthew 12:36 means "words that accomplish nothing." If God is going to judge our "small talk," how much more will He judge our deliberate words? It is by our conversation *at unguarded moments* that we reveal our true character.

RR–43

God's creation is a theater and the human mind is a picture gallery, and we link the two by using *words*.

KK–41

Work

Keeping in mind that God's concern is for the worker as well as for the work, you need to ask yourself, Where am I in my spiritual growth?

Does God still have some work to do in my life? When your service is most difficult, God may be doing His deepest work in your life, so don't run away. God uses you to build His work, but He also uses the work to build you as He prepares you for the next assignment as well as for eternal service in glory.

HH–70

Workers, Workman

If Jesus Christ had advertised for workers, the announcement might have read something like this:

"Men and women wanted for difficult task of helping to build My church. You will often be misunderstood, even by those working with you. You will face constant attack from an invisible enemy. You may not see the results of your labor, and your full reward will not come till after all your work is completed. It may cost you your home, your ambitions, even your life."

SS–210

God is more concerned about His workers than He is about their work, for if the workers are what they ought to be, the work will be what it ought to be.

A–83

The word *study* (2 Tim. 2:15) has nothing to do with books and teachers. It means "to be diligent, be zealous." It is translated in this way in 2 Timothy 4:9, 21, and also in Titus 3:12. The emphasis in this paragraph is that the workman needs to be diligent in his labors so that he will not be ashamed when his work is inspected. "Rightly dividing" means "cutting straight" and can be applied to many different tasks: plowing a straight furrow, cutting a straight board, sewing a straight seam.

SS–246

Works

There are no such categories as religious works and secular works, for the Christian is to "do all to the glory of God" (1 Cor. 10:31). The missionary doctor heals the body, that he might demonstrate God's love and eventually have the privilege of helping to heal the soul. The Christian neighbor helps those around him, not simply to win the right to be heard, but because showing Christian love is in itself a ministry to the glory of God.

DD–195

We should live godly lives and be "careful to maintain good works" (Titus 3:8). The only evidence the unsaved world has that we belong to God is our godly lives.

"Good works" do not necessarily mean religious works or church work. It is fine to work at church, sing in the choir, and hold an office; but it is also good to serve our un-saved neighbors, to be helpful in the community, and to have a reputation for assisting those in need. Baby-sitting to relieve a harassed young mother is just as much a spiritual work as passing out a gospel tract. The best way a local church has to witness to the lost is through the sacrificial service of its members.

SS–268

Works, Good

"Doing penance" without truly repenting and trusting God's mercy only multiplies the sin and deadens the conscience. Thinking they were good enough to please God, the people asked Jesus, "What shall we do, that we may work the works of God?" He replied, "This is the work of God, that you believe in Him whom He sent" (John 6:28–29 NKJV). True saving faith comes from a heart that's been broken in repentance and realizes that no amount of good works can atone for sin (Acts 20:21; 26:20; Eph. 2:8–9).

E–110

World

"The world" from a Christian point of view involves all the people, plans, organizations, activities, philosophies, values, etc. that belong to society without God. Some of these things may be very cultural; others may be very corrupt; but all of them have their origins in the heart and mind of sinful man and promote what sinful man wants to enjoy and accomplish. As Christians, we must be careful not to love the world (1 John 2:15–17) or be conformed to the world (Rom. 12:1–2).

When we trusted Christ, we moved into a new spiritual position: we are now "in Christ" and "out of the world." To be sure, we are *in* the world physically, but not *of* the world spiritually. Now that we are "partakers of the heavenly calling" (Heb. 3:1) we are no longer interested in the treasures or pleasures of sin in this world. This does not mean that we are isolated from reality or insulated from the world's needs, so "heavenly minded that we are no earthly good." Rather, it means that we look at the things of earth from heaven's point of view.

The world system functions on the basis of conformity. As long as a person follows the fads and fashions and accepts the values of the world, he or she will "get along." But the Christian refuses to be "conformed to this world" (Rom. 12:2). The believer is a "new creation" (2 Cor. 5:17) and no longer wants to live the "old life" (1 Peter 4:1–4). We are the light of the world and the salt of the earth (Matt. 5:13–16), but a dark world does not want light and a decaying world does not want salt! In other words, the believer is not just "out of step"; he is out of place! (See John 17:14, 16, and 1 John 4:5).

RR–360

Dr. A. W. Tozer used to remind us, "Every man must choose his world." True believers have "tasted the good word of God, and the powers of the world [age] to come" (Heb. 6:5); this should mean we have no interest in or appetite for the present sinful world system. Abraham chose the right world and became the father of the faithful. Lot chose the wrong world and became the father of the enemies of God's people (Gen. 19:30–38). Abraham became the friend of God (2 Chron. 20:7), but Lot became the friend of the world— and lost everything. Lot was "saved; yet so as by fire" (1 Cor. 3:15) and lost his reward.

SS–279

World, Worldliness

"If any man love the world, the love of the Father is not in him" (1 John 2:15).

Worldliness is not so much a matter of *activity* as of *attitude*. It is possible for a Christian to stay away from questionable amusements and doubtful places and still love the world, for worldliness is a matter of the heart. To the extent that a Christian loves the world system and the things in it, he does *not* love the Father.

Worldliness not only affects your response to the love of God; it also affects your response *to the will of God*. "The world passeth away . . . but he that doeth the will of God abideth forever" (1 John 2:17).

SS–492

Because the world is deceptive, it is dangerous. The world can even deceive God's own people and lead them into trouble. "Do not love the world, nor the things in the world" warned the Apostle John (1 John 2:15 NASB). "And do not be conformed to this world," wrote the Apostle Paul (Rom. 12:2 NASB). James asked the pertinent question, "Do you not know that friendship with the world is hostility toward God?" (James 4:4 NASB). "Make every effort to come to me

195

soon," Paul wrote to Timothy, "for Demas, having loved this present world, has deserted me..." (2 Tim. 4:9–10 NASB).

Satan is the prince of this world. He has declared war on God's people. "Be of sober spirit, be on the alert," Peter wrote. "Your adversary, the devil, prowls about like a roaring lion, seeking someone to devour" (1 Peter 5:8 NASB). Lions are dangerous! Satan will use the world to entice the believer out of the will of God.

We not only live in a deceived and dangerous world, but we live in a *defiled* world. The believer must be careful to keep himself "unstained by the world" (James 1:27 NASB). The new nature that we have within creates new desires and new appetites, but there are always around us the temptations to lower things. Because of this new nature, the believer has "escaped the corruption that is in the world by lust" (2 Peter 1:4 NASB); but he can still be tempted and he can still fall.

H–18

Worry

If we are to conquer worry and experience the secure mind, we must meet the conditions that God has laid down. There are three: right praying (Phil. 4:6–7), right

thinking (Phil. 4:8), and right living (Phil. 4:9).

SS–94

Wrong thinking leads to wrong feeling, and before long the heart and mind are pulled apart and we are strangled by worry. We must realize that thoughts are real and powerful, even though they cannot be seen, weighed, or measured. We must bring "into captivity every thought to the obedience of Christ" (2 Cor. 10:5).

SS–95

With the peace of God to guard us and the God of peace to guide us—*why worry?*

SS–96

Worry is an evidence of unbelief. Unbelief is an evidence of disobedience. Disobedience is an evidence that something is wrong on the inside. What is wrong? Your heart, mind, and will are possessed by things. It is not wrong to own things, but it is wrong for things to own us.

T–80

Worry is deceptive. It gives us a false view of life, of itself, and of God. Worry convinces us that life is made up of what we eat and what we wear. We get so concerned about *the means* that we totally forget about *the end,* which is to glorify God (Matt. 6:33). There is a great difference between making a living and making a life.

RR–221

Worship

Worship and service are not competitive. They always go together. When He was ministering on earth, our Lord retired to pray—then He went out to serve. We need to avoid the extremes of impractical mysticism and fleshly enthusiasm. As we spend time with God, we get to understand Him and His will for our lives; and as we go out to obey Him, we learn more.

SS–112

Whether it's evangelism, education, social action, world missions, or feeding the hungry, everything the church accomplishes for the Lord flows out of worship. If the fountainhead of worship is polluted, the church's entire ministry will be defiled. Like the Jews in Amos's day, we're only going to Bethel and sinning! Therefore, it behooves God's people to examine their hearts and make certain that their motives are right and that what they do in public meetings glorifies the Lord.

E–39

The late Dr. A. W. Tozer once wrote: "I can safely say on the authority of all that is revealed in the Word of God that any man or woman on this earth who is bored and turned off by worship is not ready for heaven." I think Dr. Tozer was correct. Heaven is a place of worship, and if you and I cannot endure a time of worshiping God here on earth, what are we going to do when we get to heaven? Perhaps the greatest lack in our churches today is in the area of worship.

NN–15

Worship is the most important activity of a local church family. Ministry must flow out of worship, otherwise it becomes busy activity without power and without heart. There may be "results," but they will not glorify God or really last. Many church services lack an emphasis on true worship and are more like religious entertainments, catering to the appetites of the congregation.

SS–189

I'm convinced that everything the church is supposed to do in this world is a by-product of spiritual worship, and that includes evangelism, missions, giving, works of mercy, education, and personal holiness and service. First God calls

197

us to worship, then He sends us out to witness and to work. God wants worship to come first, for only then will we be energized by His power and bring glory to His name. Worship puts God where He deserves to be and keeps man where he ought to be. But in the worship of the Great God Entertainment, man gets the glory, and God gets lost in the fun.

WW–47

In today's language, "Keep thy foot!" means "Watch your step!" Even though God's glorious presence doesn't dwell in our church buildings as it did in the temple, believers today still need to heed the warning. *The worship of God is the highest ministry of the church and must come from devoted hearts and yielded wills.* For God's people to participate in public worship while harboring unconfessed sin is to ask for God's rebuke and judgment (Isa. 1:10–20; Amos 5; Ps. 50).

N–64

Our worship must be balanced. If we only exalt God, and extol His greatness and holiness, we may isolate Him from man and his needs. On the other hand, if we fail to exalt Him and recognize that He is "high and holy," we will be prone to bring Him down to our level and treat Him with undue familiarity. The theologians call this the "tension between the transcendence and the immanence of God." Of course, the "tension" is solved by the Incarnation of Jesus Christ; He is "Emmanuel . . . God with us" (Matt. 1:23). Our God is so great, that He is high above us and yet *right with us* at the same time!

GG–19

Y

Yield

The word *yield* is found five times in this section (Rom. 6:13, 16, and 19), and means "to place at one's disposal, to present, to offer as a sacrifice." According to Romans 12:1, the believer's body should be presented to the Lord as "a living sacrifice" for His glory. The Old Testament sacrifices were dead sacrifices. The Lord may ask some of us to die for Him, but He asks all of us to *live* for Him.

How we are to yield (vv. 12–13). This is an act of the will based on the knowledge we have of what Christ has done for us. It is an intelligent act—not the impulsive decision of the moment based on some emotional stirring. It is important to notice the tenses of the verbs in these verses. A literal translation is: "Do not constantly allow sin to reign in your mortal body so that you are constantly obeying its lusts. Neither constantly yield your members of your body as weapons [or tools] of unrighteousness to sin; but once and for all yield yourselves to God." That once-and-for-all surrender is described in Romans 12:1.

There must be in the believer's life that final and complete surrender of the body to Jesus Christ. This does not mean there will be no further steps of surrender, because there will be. The longer we walk with Christ, the deeper the fellowship must become. But there can be no subsequent steps without that first step. The tense of the verb in Romans 12:1 corresponds with that in Romans 6:13—a once-and-for-all yielding to the Lord. To be sure, we daily surrender afresh to Him; but even that is based on a final and complete surrender.

RR–163

As the believer yields to Christ in daily experience, he enjoys "the peace of God" in his heart and mind (Phil. 4:6–7).

RR–191

Each of us must decide whether we will go through life *pretending*, like Judas; or *fighting*, like Peter; or *yielding to God's perfect will*, like Jesus. Will it be the kiss, the sword, or the cup? (John 18:1–11).

RR–270

Yoke

The yoke that He gives us is tailor-made. He knows exactly how we feel, and He knows just what we can take. He says, "I am going to be yoked with you. *Together* we are going to teach that Sunday school class. *Together* we are going to raise those precious children. *Together* we are going to pastor that church or work in that mission field." We are yoked with the Lord Jesus. This means we can carry burdens and still have rest in our hearts.

EE–84

Z

Zeal, Zealous

Ever since Israel returned to their land from Babylonian Captivity, the nation had been cured of idolatry. In the temple and the local synagogues, only the true God was worshiped and served, and only the true Law was taught. So zealous were the Jews that they even "improved upon God's Law" and added their own traditions, making them equal to the Law. Paul himself had been zealous for the Law and the traditions (Acts 26:1–11; Gal. 1:13–14).

But their zeal was not based on knowledge; it was heat without light. Sad to say, many religious people today are making the same mistake. They think that their good works and religious deeds will save them, when actually these practices are keeping them from being saved. Certainly many of them are sincere and devout, but sincerity and devotion will never save the soul. "Therefore by the deeds of the law there shall no flesh be justified in his sight" (Rom. 3:20).

RR–546–47

201

SCRIPTURE INDEX

204

205

Warren W. Wiersbe is Distinguished Professor of Preaching at Grand Rapids Baptist Seminary and has pastored churches in Indiana, Kentucky, and Illinois (Chicago's historic Moody Church). He is the author of more than one hundred books, including *God Isn't in a Hurry, The Bumps Are What You Climb On,* and *The Bible Exposition Commentary* (2 vols.).

James R. Adair joined the editorial staff of Scripture Press Publications, Inc., in 1945 after three years as a newspaper reporter in Asheville, North Carolina. Until 1975 he served as editor of Power for Living and other Scripture Press Sunday school take-home papers. In 1972 he became founding director of the company's Victor Books Division. He worked for Scripture Press for fifty-one years, during which time he authored or coauthored seven books and compiled eleven others.